A New Way

Introducing Higher Education to Professional Learning Communities at Work™

Robert Eaker   Debra Sells

Solution Tree | Press

a division of
Solution Tree

555 North Morton Street
Bloomington, IN 47404
800.733.6786 (toll free) / 812.336.7700
FAX: 812.336.7790

email: info@solution-tree.com
solution-tree.com

Printed in the United States of America

19   18   17   16   15   1   2   3   4   5

Library of Congress Cataloging-in-Publication Data

Eaker, Robert E.

A new way : introducing higher education to professional learning communities at work / Robert Eaker and Debra Sells.

   pages cm

Includes bibliographical references and index.

ISBN 978-1-942496-29-8 (perfect bound) 1. Professional learning communities--United States. 2. College teachers--In-service training--United States. 3. Educational leadership--United States. 4. Universities and colleges--Administration--United States. 5. Education, Higher--Aims and objectives--United States. I. Sells, Debra. II. Title.

   LB1738.E246 2016

   378.1'2--dc23

                              2015030154

Solution Tree
Jeffrey C. Jones, CEO
Edmund M. Ackerman, President

Solution Tree Press
President: Douglas M. Rife
Senior Acquisitions Editor: Amy Rubenstein
Editorial Director: Lesley Bolton
Managing Production Editor: Caroline Weiss
Copy Editor: Miranda Addonizio
Proofreader: Ashante K. Thomas
Text and Cover Designer: Rian Anderson
Compositor: Abigail Bowen

To Star

My wife for over four decades, and whose encouragement, enthusiasm, patience, and support made this book a reality.

—Bob

To Alice

You were right—and I am grateful!

—Deb

Acknowledgments

———

Our thinking undergirding *A New Way* has been influenced by educators who are leading the call for the reform of our institutions of higher education, including Derek Bok, Michael Barber, Robert Barr and John Tagg, Richard Arum and Josipa Roksa, and Vincent Tinto, to name a few. Our belief that the concepts and practices of professional learning communities offer our best hope for enhancing student success at the college and university level has been greatly influenced by the pioneering work of Richard DuFour and Becky DuFour. To these educators and many others, we are grateful.

A major impetus for this book has been our work with the administrators, faculty, and staff at Middle Tennessee State University (MTSU), who have embarked on a journey to significantly enhance student retention and graduation rates. We would like to acknowledge the contributions they have made to our work and our thinking about leading organizational change in order to enhance student learning and success. Additionally, Dr. Jim Rund of Arizona State University (ASU) has been a friend and mentor to Deb for nearly thirty years. Jim has been generous in sharing the innovative approaches to student success being taken at his institution; the ASU approach proves student success strategies can be successfully scaled up to even the largest universities.

Of special significance to our efforts has been the leadership, dedication, and persistence of MTSU's president, Dr. Sidney McPhee. Not only has Dr. McPhee tirelessly led the numerous re-culturing efforts across every level of our university, he has graciously supported us and our work. His encouragement is greatly appreciated.

All authors should be so fortunate to have a publisher that is as professional, supportive, and generous as Solution Tree Press. Our special thanks and gratitude go to Douglas Rife, the president of Solution Tree Press, and our editor, Lesley Bolton, as well as the numerous other individuals at Solution Tree who have worked so hard to make this book come to life. Simply put, this book would not have been possible without them.

Finally, we acknowledge Jeff Jones, the co-owner and chief executive officer of Solution Tree. Jeff has been Bob's dear friend for over seventeen years and has published each of his books since 1998. Jeff's passion for and commitment to improving education worldwide and his dedication to Solution Tree authors is evident in everything that happens at Solution Tree. From the initial thoughts about this book to publication, Jeff has been encouraging and enthusiastic in his support, and for that, and his friendship, we are very grateful.

Table of Contents

CHAPTER 3

Leading Cultural Change 37

CHAPTER 4

Enhancing Student Success Through a Commitments-Driven University 51

CHAPTER 5

Capturing the Power of Collaborative Teaming 69

CHAPTER 6

Enhancing Student Success in a Culture of Continuous Improvement

CHAPTER 7

Bridging the Rhetoric-Reality Gap: Helping More Students Succeed—As If We Really Mean It 127

CHAPTER 8

Improving Student Retention and Graduation Rates: The Undergraduate Experience 145

CHAPTER 9

Overcoming Barriers: Roadblocks, Detours, and Occasional Breakdowns 181

EPILOGUE

A New Normal. 193

References and Resources 197

Index 207

About the Authors

Robert Eaker, EdD, is professor emeritus at Middle Tennessee State University, where he also served as dean of the College of Education and later as interim executive vice president and provost. Dr. Eaker is a former fellow with the National Center for Effective Schools Research and Development.

He has written widely on the issues of effective teaching, effective schools, helping teachers use research findings, and high expectations for student achievement, and he has co-authored with Richard and Rebecca DuFour numerous books and other resources on the topic of re-culturing schools and school districts into professional learning communities.

In 1998, Dr. Eaker was recognized by the governor of Tennessee as a recipient of Tennessee's Outstanding Achievement Award. Also, in 1998, the Tennessee House of Representatives passed a proclamation recognizing him for his dedication and commitment to the field of education. In 2003, Dr. Eaker was selected by the Middle Tennessee State University Student Government Association to receive the Womack Distinguished Faculty Award.

For over four decades, Dr. Eaker has served as a consultant to school districts throughout North America and has been a frequent speaker at state, regional, and national meetings.

 **Debra Sells, EdD,** serves as vice president for student affairs and vice provost for enrollment services at Middle Tennessee State University. She has served as an administrator at a variety of colleges and universities over her career of more than thirty years, including Grinnell College, California Polytechnic State University in San Luis Obispo, and Arizona State University. Along with Bob Eaker, Debra has co-authored previous articles and chapters about academic and student affairs collaboration in higher education and on the application of professional learning community concepts and practices to colleges and universities.

To book Robert Eaker or Debra Sells for professional development, contact pd@solution-tree.com.

Introduction

———

The story of the United States is perhaps most often told as one of success achieved through hard work and education. The twin admonitions to "work hard" and "get a good education" have always formed the foundation of America's promise of upward mobility. In today's high-tech and global economy, postsecondary education is perhaps more important than ever. A Federal Reserve Bank of New York study confirms the importance of a college degree, emphasizing that those who fail to complete an undergraduate degree are falling further and further behind in the economic playing field. As Jaison Abel and Richard Deitz (2014), the authors of the study, note, "Average wages for those with a college degree are far greater than average wages for those with only a high school diploma" (p. 2). They conclude that workers with a bachelor's degree can expect to earn approximately one million dollars more than non–college graduates during their lifetimes, despite rising tuition costs.

Clearly, Americans see a college education as one of the prerequisites for upward mobility. Because it is so important, increasing access to a quality education has been a consistent theme throughout U.S. history. The movement to enhance access to education has progressed from the earliest Latin grammar schools to elementary education for all, to universal secondary education, to the establishment of public land-grant institutions, to the GI Bill, to the formation of the community-college system, to the implementation of the Pell Grant program—to name just a few historic milestones aimed at increasing access to education.

However, better access to postsecondary education does not always correlate with improved student success. Despite efforts to increase the number of students attending U.S. colleges and universities, graduation rates remain stagnant—hovering around 50 percent. Moreover, in spite of significant tuition increases at public colleges and universities, graduation rates have remained largely unchanged, causing many to question whether higher education leaders are truly committed to enhancing student success.

The fact is, university leaders are committed to student success. Most colleges and universities offer at least a few tutoring programs for students who are struggling. And it is not unusual for colleges and universities to provide math labs or reading labs to assist students. One only has to look at the efforts that are made to increase retention rates for student athletes to realize that presidents of institutions of higher education recognize the importance of enhancing student success. The issue is not the need to convince administrators, faculty, and staff of higher education institutions that raising retention and graduation rates is a worthy goal, but rather to develop an effective strategy to give them the means to re-culture their institutions in order to enhance student success. There is good news, however; more is known about how to improve organizations of all types, especially learning organizations, than ever before.

One of the most powerful tools for enhancing student success rates is the professional learning community (PLC) concept. There is virtually unanimous agreement among researchers and practitioners on the power of PLC concepts and practices to improve organizations in which student and adult learning is at the core of enterprise. Professional literature abounds with evidence for the positive effects of embedding PLC concepts and practices, and virtually every major educational organization in the United States, such as the National Education Association, supports their implementation. The PLC concept holds great promise for reshaping how leaders of higher education institutions think, how they work, and more important, how well students succeed.

This book is written as a guide to implement the concepts and practices of professional learning communities in colleges and universities. These concepts and practices are applicable to virtually any organization—especially other learning organizations, such as elementary and secondary schools, but also organizations in a broad range of fields, such as health care, social services, human resource management, and governmental services. The concepts and practices intrinsic to the PLC framework provide a model that is inherently doable, grounded in research-based practices, and requires little, if any, additional resource expenditures.

This book also has special significance for those who prepare teachers to serve in U.S. schools. Of the approximate 120 semester hours that a typical teacher education student will take pursuing an undergraduate degree, only a small portion is taught by college of education faculty. Teacher education students take the vast majority of their classes in other colleges. Prospective teachers are impacted by the instructional modeling they encounter *in all of their coursework combined*; for good or for ill, students training to become teachers learn about their chosen profession from *every* professor in *every* class. In short, institutions of higher education should model the very best practices throughout the university every day, in every classroom, in every office, with every interaction, with every student—but especially with students who will become teachers.

The term *professional learning communities* has become so popular that many people use it in varying ways, for differing purposes, to the point that it's essentially meaningless. Because the term is so widespread, we want to be clear about its meaning in this book; we use the PLC concept and practices based on the work of Richard DuFour and Robert Eaker (1998) in *Professional Learning Communities at Work*, and Richard DuFour, Rebecca DuFour, and Robert Eaker (2008) in *Revisiting Professional Learning Communities at Work*. In subsequent chapters, we use the term *professional learning communities* sparingly. Instead, we emphasize the concepts and practices reflective of a professional learning community.

In chapter 1, "Enhancing Student Success With the Promise of Professional Learning Communities," we clarify what PLCs are—and equally important, what they are not—and highlight the potential of the concept and related practices for institutions of higher education seeking to make a significant and systemic impact on student retention and graduation rates.

U.S. higher education institutions—particularly public colleges and universities—are experiencing an avalanche of criticism on a number of fronts. One area of public frustration stems from the fact that although historically there have been significant initiatives aimed at enhancing access to higher education, corollary increases in student completion rates have not matched the increased access. Chapter 2, "The Journey From Student Access to Student Success," highlights the major efforts and milestones designed to increase student access to higher education, along with a synthesis of the mounting criticisms of higher education, and points to current demands for major changes in the very culture of public higher education institutions—how they perform and how student success rates must improve.

Higher education institutions will need to make a number of structural changes—in terms of roles, responsibilities, policies, and procedures—in order to enhance student success rates. However, structural changes, by themselves, will not be enough. The more difficult challenge facing colleges and universities is making the requisite cultural changes in the beliefs, values, attitudes, and habits that constitute the norm of university life—literally, how things are done. While there is no one right way to change organizational culture, one indispensable factor is strong, effective, passionate, and persistent leadership. Therefore chapter 3, "Leading Cultural Change," focuses on the actions leaders can take to successfully guide structural and cultural changes within their institutions and enhance student success.

While it is essential that leaders work together to develop and communicate a clear and compelling purpose, as well as a vision of what they seek to achieve, the engine that drives cultural change in organizations is a set of collaboratively developed, clearly articulated, and constantly monitored commitments. In chapter 4, "Enhancing Student Success Through a Commitments-Driven University," we describe how leaders go beyond discussions about "what we believe" to "what we are prepared to do" in order to be more successful with more students.

Collaborative teams are the driving force of successful organizations in the 21st century. Collaborative teaming has become the norm in virtually every major organization throughout the world. Yet many—if not most—colleges and universities still cling to a culture of professional isolation. Chapter 5, "Capturing the Power of Collaborative Teaming," not only highlights the power of collaborative teaming but also describes how leaders can impact what teams actually do, day in and day out, in order to positively influence student retention and graduation rates.

College and university administrators, faculty, and staff must undertake specific actions to enhance student success, but it is equally important that leaders see the big picture—that they have the ability to connect the dots. Unless they can envision improvement through an overarching conceptual framework, efforts to raise student retention and success rates will appear to be a series of disconnected initiatives or unrelated events. Chapter 6, "Enhancing Student Success in a Culture of Continuous Improvement," describes how leaders can implement a data-based, collaborative approach that serves as a way of thinking about improving student success throughout the university environment.

Chapter 7, "Bridging the Reality-Rhetoric Gap: Helping More Students Succeed—As If We Really Mean It," addresses the gap between the rhetoric of supporting student success and the stark reality of retention and graduation data. And chapter 8, "Improving Student Retention and Graduation Rates: The Undergraduate Experience," describes successful best practices that a number of institutions are implementing to improve student success.

Implementing PLC concepts and practices, if done effectively and with fidelity, can positively impact student success. However, re-culturing any organization, particularly institutions of higher education, is a complex, difficult, and incremental undertaking. Chapter 9, "Overcoming Barriers: Roadblocks, Detours, and Occasional Breakdowns," addresses the potential barriers that college and university leaders are likely to face as they engage in the challenging work of culture change—and offers suggestions for overcoming them.

Organizational culture can be understood, at least in part, through the stories its participants tell. The epilogue contains the story of Ray Kuntz and his calculus professor, Al Murray. His narrative starkly contrasts with the rather tired and demeaning one that often describes (astonishingly, sometimes with pride!) one's higher education experience: "Our professor told us, 'Look to your left. Now, look to your right. Only one of you will still be here at the end of the course!'" College and university leaders who successfully embed PLC concepts and practices can write new stories—stories of student success, rather than failure, and stories that motivate and inspire, rather than discourage and humiliate. We know enough about what colleges and universities should do, as well as what they should stop doing. The issue is not a lack of knowledge. The needs of higher education are the same needs of all large enterprises—high-quality leadership, data-based decision making, passion and persistence, and the courage to choose to create a new normal in which stories like Ray Kuntz's are the rule, rather than the exception.

The future of higher education in the United States is yet to be written. We have to begin making the necessary changes now. We must not wait until the time is right. The time will never be right. We cannot wait until everyone is on board; we will never have everyone on board. Instead, we must turn to the very core of effective leadership and choose to act! To quote Martin Luther King Jr.:

> We are confronted with the fierce urgency of now. In the unfolding conundrum of life and history there is such a thing as being too late. Procrastination is still the thief of time. We must move past indecision to action. Now, let us begin. The choice is ours, and though we may prefer it otherwise, we must choose in this crucial moment of human history. (as cited in Carson & Shepherd, 2001, p. 163)

Most important, we hope this book will be a helpful tool for those who are committed to helping more students succeed in their college experience. The concepts and practices reflective of a high-performing professional learning community hold tremendous potential for positively changing the culture of institutions of higher education. The issue isn't one of a lack of knowledge, but rather one of leadership and will. The time to act is now. The vision of enhanced student success can become more than a slogan. It can become a reality.

CHAPTER 1

Enhancing Student Success With the Promise of Professional Learning Communities

There is one thing stronger than all the armies in the world, and that is an idea whose time has come.

—Victor Hugo

With a nod to Bob Dylan, "The times they are a-changin'"—especially for faculty and administrators of public colleges and universities in the United States. State legislatures, business communities, politicians, parents, and students are becoming increasingly vocal in expressing their dissatisfaction with the one thing that is *not* changing in higher education. In spite of research on student success dating back to the 1960s, not to mention unprecedented tuition increases since 2005, student completion rates have remained stagnant, hovering around 50 percent. Stakeholders are calling into question the commitment to enhancing student success rates of those in charge of our colleges and universities—and perhaps rightly so. What other business or industry is able to survive in the marketplace with a failure rate so high?

Graduation rates aren't the only target of frustration. One only has to read the papers to find headlines highlighting U.S. grievances with everything from the loan burden of college graduates to skyrocketing salaries for coaches and budgets for athletic departments. A common theme of the dissatisfaction is the unsustainable costs of higher education. Stacy Khadaroo (2010), writing in the *Christian Science Monitor*, notes, "For more than 20 years, the costs of college have risen even more than those of healthcare" (p. 9). Americans no longer buy the argument that higher costs translate into a higher quality experience—or into greater student success.

University professors and administrators have offered their own critiques on the state of U.S. colleges and universities. In books with titles such as *The Moral Collapse of the University*, *The Closing of the American Mind*, *Profscam*, *The University in Ruins*, *Killing the Spirit*, *War Against the Intellect*, and *Our Underachieving Colleges*, they have expressed criticisms ranging from dissatisfaction with the state of higher education curricula to what some view as the lowering of intellectual standards. In each case, however, the overarching perception is consistent: the state of U.S. colleges and universities—particularly undergraduate education—is in disarray.

Many critics, particularly within the business community, deride the quality of the preparation of the 50 percent of students who do actually graduate. They generally express this criticism with complaints about a perceived disconnect between the skills and knowledge students acquire in their degree programs and the demands of the job market. They point out that higher education institutions have attempted to meet the perceived needs of employers by focusing their attention on new professional majors and degree programs and on the creation of massive open online courses (MOOCs) taught by the most respected academics in a given field, and by providing evidence of achievement to employers through grades and standardized test scores.

Meanwhile, employers indicate their real needs are for graduates who have developed more generalized and transferable thinking, problem-solving, and communication skills. Robert J. Sternberg (2013), writing in *The Chronicle of Higher Education*, notes that employers "tell us that creative, critical, practical and wisdom-based decision-making and problem-solving skills, along with a mindset of lifelong learning and a strong work ethic, are far more important than current fads in the literature" (p. 10).

Ironically, while some critics attack public colleges and universities for the lack of job preparation exhibited by their graduates, others deride them for increasingly becoming mere job-training institutions, lacking the academic rigor of a traditional classic education. In their attempts to respond to both lines of criticism, colleges and universities have opened themselves to the accusation that they have no focus, no true identity—that they are trying to be everything for everyone.

Dissatisfaction within the business community translates into pressure on the political establishment to effect change. Increasingly, state legislatures insist that public colleges and universities demonstrate measurable improvements in student academic success. Many states are responding by rewriting funding formulas that connect state financial support to graduation rates. In short, the same waves of accountability measures aimed at K–12 public schools beginning with the No Child Left Behind legislation now lap at the shores of U.S. public institutions of higher education.

Through a New Lens: Colleges and Universities as PLCs

Naturally, given the increased accountability demands of state legislatures, leaders of public institutions of higher education are struggling to find ways to improve student completion rates. This is no easy task. However, they would be wise to consider those approaches that other education leaders find successful. K–12 schools that effectively met the challenge of the No Child Left Behind legislation can provide examples of the structural and cultural changes necessary to significantly improve student success in higher education.

The rather remarkable change in U.S. K–12 schools since the mid-2000s is tied to the student success model that has come to be known in education as the professional learning community movement. In fact, schools throughout North America—and increasingly around the world—have shown dramatic increases in student achievement by adopting these concepts and practices. Rarely in U.S. history has there been such widespread agreement on how to improve virtually all organizations, especially those with a core purpose of learning.

Researchers and practitioners alike have endorsed the concepts and practices inherent in the PLC framework, as has virtually every major educational organization and commission. Businesses and other complex organizations such as the Mayo Clinic, Nissan Motor Corporation, Federal Express, Volvo, and the Dana Corporation have successfully applied the concepts, as well. Although they may not all use the term *professional learning community*, organizations in industry, health care, education, and other fields have increased their effectiveness with the particular combination of concepts, priorities, and practices that form the basis of the PLC model. Consider the following examples of support for the PLC concept as cited by DuFour, DuFour, and Eaker (2008, pp. 68, 69, 70, 72).

> The most successful corporation of the future will be a learning organization. (Senge, 1990, p. 4)

> The new problem of change . . . is what would it take to make the educational system a learning organization—expert at dealing with change as a normal part of its work, not just in relation to the latest policy, but as a way of life. (Fullan, 1993, p. 4)

> If schools want to enhance their organizational capacity to boost student learning, they should work on building a professional community that is characterized by shared purpose, collaborative activity, and collective responsibility among staff. (Newmann & Wehlage, 1995, p. 37)

We support and encourage the use of professional learning communities (PLCs) as a central element for effective
professional development and a comprehensive reform
initiative. In our experience, PLCs have the potential to
enhance the professional culture within a school district.
(Annenberg Institute for School Reform, 2004, p. 3)

The framework of a professional learning community is
inextricably linked to the effective integration of standards, assessment, and accountability. . . . The leaders of
professional learning communities balance the desire for
professional autonomy with the fundamental principles
and values that drive collaboration and mutual accountability. (Reeves, 2005, pp. 47–48)

[In the most successful schools] leadership ensures there
are integrated communities of professional practice in the
service of student academic and social learning. There is
a healthy school environment in which student learning is the central focus. . . . Research has demonstrated
that schools organized as communities, rather than bu-
reaucracies, are more likely to exhibit academic success.
(Goldring, Porter, Murphy, Elliott, & Cravens, 2007)

Such a tipping point—from reform to true collaboration—could represent the most dramatic shift in the
history of educational practice . . . We will know we have
succeeded when the absence of a "strong professional
learning community" in a school is an embarrassment.
(Schmoker, 2004a, p. 431)

PLCs and How They Work

What is a professional learning community? Answering this question is difficult. The question implies that a PLC is a thing—a static
object. However, at the most basic level, a PLC is simply a way of
thinking—a way of doing things within an organization, day in,
day out. In other words, the term *professional learning community*
describes an organizational *culture*—the collective beliefs, attitudes,
and habits that constitute the norm.

Michael Fullan (2005) reminds us that "terms travel easily . . . but the meaning of the underlying concept does not" (p. 67). As an idea gains popularity, it is only natural that increasing numbers of writers, researchers, and practitioners offer their views, findings, and insights on it. Definitions and descriptions can become confusing, if not outright contradictory. Richard DuFour, Rebecca DuFour, Robert Eaker, and Thomas Many (2010) reflect on this issue:

> It has been interesting to observe the growing popularity of the term *professional learning community*. In fact, the term has become so commonplace and has been used so ambiguously to describe virtually any loose coupling of individuals who share a common interest in education that it is in danger of losing all meaning. (p. 10)

There is an increasing array of books, articles, blogs, and opinions related to the PLC concept. To be clear, as mentioned in the introduction, the concepts and practices that we propose for improved student learning, and hence completion rates in public higher education institutions, are based on the framework described by DuFour and Eaker (1998) in *Professional Learning Communities at Work* and in *Revisiting Professional Learning Communities at Work* (DuFour et al., 2008).

All of the practices of any professional learning community—whether applied to education, business, or health care—are built on a framework of three fundamental ideas. Despite their simplicity, these ideas reflect major cultural shifts in how complex organizations, in particular, go about their work. If colleges and universities are to enhance student success significantly, they must not only develop a deep, rich understanding of the implications of each of these ideas but also demonstrate a passionate and persistent commitment to embed these ideas in every aspect of institutional culture.

The First Big Idea: An Intense Focus on Learning

In *Good to Great*, Jim Collins (2001) artfully illustrates the concept underlying the first big idea of a professional learning community.

In his chapters "The Hedgehog Concept" and "A Culture of Discipline," Collins emphasizes the absolute necessity for high-performing organizations to focus relentlessly and consistently on the core of the business—for leaders to pursue with discipline the one big thing they can do better than anyone else and not be distracted by competing priorities and interests.

How do these ideas apply to higher education? This is discussed in more detail later, but for now, suffice it to note that the first big idea of a PLC in educational organizations—the idea upon which all the basic assumptions and practices should rest—is that the core focus must be on student *learning*. In a PLC, the focus shifts fundamentally from making sure courses are *taught* to ensuring that students, in fact, *learn*. When educational institutions make enhancing learning for all students the core mission—the very reason for existence—and really mean it, they affect virtually every aspect of the organization, both structurally and culturally.

While K–12 schools embrace this shift in focus from teaching—that is, covering content—to student learning, increasingly there is recognition of the need for institutions of higher education to embrace the same shift. Robert Barr and John Tagg (1995) note:

> We are beginning to recognize that our dominant paradigm mistakes a means for an end. It takes the means or method—called "instruction" or "teaching"—and makes it the college's end or purpose. To say that the purpose of colleges is to provide instruction is like saying that General Motors' business is to operate assembly lines or that the purpose of medical care is to fill hospital beds. We now see that our mission is not instruction but rather that of producing *learning* with every student by *whatever* means work best. . . . The Learning Paradigm also opens up the truly inspiring goal that each graduating class learns more than the previous graduating class. In other words, the Learning Paradigm envisions the institution itself as a learner—over time, it continuously

learns how to produce more learning with each graduating class, each entering student. (p. 13)

While shifting from a culture of teaching to a culture of learning may at first seem like a simple idea—one that has the ring of a
cliché—the implications of such a shift are enormous. Colleges and
universities that successfully make this shift will ask different fundamental questions regarding their mission, goals, and operations,
and more important, they will act in fundamentally different ways.

The Second Big Idea: Capturing the Power of Collaborative Teaming

The use of high-performing collaborative teaming is not unique
to K–12 reform or even to the PLC model. It is the central organizing principle found in effective organizations of virtually all kinds
throughout the world. Since at least the early 1990s, researchers
and experts in organizational development have touted the power
of high-performing teams. Jeffrey Pfeffer and Robert Sutton (2000)
observe, "Interdependence is what organizations are all about.
Productivity, performance, and innovation result from joint action,
not just individual efforts and behavior" (p. 197).

In fact, collaborative teaming is so widely used that it has become
a way of life in most organizations—except in higher education.
It's been said that colleges and universities are a collection of independent contractors connected by a common parking lot. Such a
comment may exaggerate, but at their most basic level, traditional
college and university structures represent a culture of isolation—
individual professors left on their own to teach the students they
are assigned. Professional learning communities represent the exact
opposite. A PLC can best be described as a community with a collaborative culture, in which teams work together to help all students
learn. DuFour et al. (2010) define the collaborative culture of a PLC
when they write, "In a professional learning community, *collaboration* represents a systematic process in which teachers work together

interdependently in order to *impact* their classroom practice in ways that will lead to better results for their students" (p. 12).

PLCs go beyond merely inviting or encouraging collaboration. They *embed* a collaborative culture within the day-to-day life of the institution by organizing administrators, faculty, and staff into collaborative teams. Collaborative teams, and the work they do, are the power source of a PLC. Although the teams direct their work toward the common goal of the institution—ensuring the learning of all students—within these parameters, teams have autonomy and are encouraged to experiment. The primary question facing each team is, Are your students being demonstrably successful? Effective teams are relentless in helping more students learn more, and the team members hold each other mutually accountable for results. In short, teams accept collective responsibility for student success and continually seek to improve their own performance as well as the performance of their students.

The Third Big Idea: A Focus on Results

In *Results-Based Leadership*, Dave Ulrich, Jack Zenger, and Norman Smallwood (1999) shift the conversation about what constitutes great leaders away from the dominant paradigm, which traditionally has been a focus on the inner, personal characteristics and attributes of leaders. Instead, as its title suggests, the authors propose, quite simply, that the hallmark of effective leaders is that they ultimately get results.

> In the search for more effective leadership, something has often been overlooked. Being capable and possessing the attributes of leadership is terrific, but capability must be put to appropriate, purposeful use. Our message to leaders may be put into the simple formula *Effective leadership = attributes x results.* (p. 3)

Often, when a traditional college and university culture undertakes the implementation of a new initiative or idea, the question faculty and staff often ask of leaders is, "How do you like it?" Obviously, the feelings of faculty and staff working within an institution may impact motivation and effectiveness and should not be ignored, but in a PLC, the happiness of adults is not the *primary* focus. Leaders of organizations that function as PLCs focus relentlessly on results related to the primary goal. In the case of educational institutions, the question is, How has this effort affected student learning? Leaders shift the institutional emphasis from intentions to results.

In a PLC, collaborative teams of professors and others continually analyze multiple sources of data. Using the results of their own data analysis, they reflect on the effectiveness of their professional practice. They seek to gain deeper understanding of ways to continuously improve student performance and success. In this way, the learning of administrators, faculty, and staff enhances the learning of students. Most important, they set *meaningful* improvement goals. Since teams constantly experiment with new ways to increase their effectiveness, they create a broader university culture of continuous improvement. In fact, the key to understanding the power of professional learning communities is to understand the power of mutual accountability for *results*.

Summary

Despite approximately fifty years of research and concern about low student retention and success at the university level, graduation rates remain stubbornly stuck at around 50 percent. And this is in spite of significant tuition increases over the past decade. Is there another industry in which such limited success would be tolerated? Not surprisingly, the pressure that was brought to bear on K–12 public education is now being aimed at our colleges and universities.

Is there a proven, cost-effective way for colleges and universities to significantly improve retention and graduation rates? The good news is that the answer to this question is a resounding "Yes!" The professional learning community concept—with its emphasis on student learning, the use of high-performing teams, and a passionate and persistent focus on results—offers university leaders powerful, proven tools for enhancing student success.

Practices reflective of the PLC concept are found in all types of organizations across the globe. Many highly successful companies, government agencies, and the military have captured the power of the PLC concept and its inherent practices. The practices of a professional learning community, unfortunately, are less frequently found in institutions of higher education where practices still reflect, to a large degree, professional isolation rather than collaboration, a focus on presenting content rather than ensuring learning, and intentions rather than results. With the increased expectation that colleges and universities improve retention and graduation rates, the time has come for institutions of higher education to capture the power of the professional learning community concept. The need is greater than ever. The time is right, and the path is clearly marked. It is time for the journey to begin!

CHAPTER 2

The Journey From Student Access to Student Success

Deep, radical and urgent transformation is required in higher education. The biggest risk is that as a result of complacency, caution or anxiety the pace of change is too slow and the nature of change too incremental. The modes of higher education that marched triumphantly across the globe in the second half of the 20th century are broken. . . .

The mountainside looks solid indeed, but there are changes "under the surface." They are "rather invisible," but they are unmistakable. An avalanche is coming. It's hard, of course, to say exactly when. It may be sooner than we think. Certainly there is no better time than now to seek to understand what lies ahead for higher education—and to prepare.

—Michael Barber, Katelyn Donnelly, and Saad Rivi

From its earliest colonial days, the United States has been a destination for people from across the globe driven by the hope of a better life, both economically and socially. While pursuing the American dream has meant different things to different individuals and groups at different times in our history, Americans consistently view education as an essential prerequisite to achieving their goals. Even more important, Americans believe education is a cornerstone for a democratic society. Franklin D. Roosevelt (2010) echoed this view in 1938 when he said, "Democracy cannot succeed unless those who express their choice are prepared to choose wisely. The real safeguard of democracy, therefore, is education" (p. 17).

Perhaps more than ever, the 21st century world requires more and better education and a dramatically different view of higher education than the more traditional one that governed the structures and cultures of colleges and universities of the past. Today, we live in a world where knowledge and information are growing exponentially and where technological innovation expands at an astounding rate. Increased automation in the workforce is eliminating many routine jobs, meaning some sort of postsecondary training or education is increasingly necessary. Multiple career changes are a fact of life for most Americans, making lifelong learning a necessity. Not only do we live in a global economic community, but political struggles in places thousands of miles away may have immediate impact close to home. Issues relating to resources and the environment require collective action from people around the globe.

And yet, dissatisfaction with U.S. higher education is so intense that a new wave of books and articles question whether or not increased participation and investment in a four-year degree program is necessary or even desirable. Despite evidence that Americans who hold college degrees earn, on average, substantially more across their lifetimes than non–degree holders and that four-year degree holders experience lower rates of unemployment during economic downturns, there is a growing sense of skepticism. Even such notable authorities as William Bennett, former U.S. secretary of education, are asking the nagging question, Is college worth it? Bennett (2013) is less than enthusiastic about our increasing investment in higher education relative to what he sees as a paltry payoff, noting, "The truth is that too many people are going to college. . . . College, as currently apprised, should not be a universal commodity" (p. xiii).

The report of the Wingspread Group on Higher Education, *An American Imperative: Higher Expectations for Higher Education*, foreshadowed the need for the creation of a new lens through which to view higher education in the United States (Johnson Foundation, 1993). The report issued the following warning:

> A disturbing and dangerous mismatch exists between what American society needs of higher education and what it is receiving. Nowhere is the mismatch more dangerous than in the quality of undergraduate preparation provided on many campuses. The American imperative for the 21st century is that society must hold higher education to much higher standards or risk national decline. (p. 1)

A 2011 article by Karen Fischer in *The Chronicle of Higher Education* trumpeted American concerns in the title: "Crisis of Confidence Threatens Colleges." In the article, Stephen R. Portch, former chancellor of the University System of Georgia, declares, "We're staring fundamental change in the face. Our system is bankrupt, and we've got to have a new model."

Access for a Few

The mistrust of a college degree's value is a relatively recent phenomenon in the landscape of higher education development in the United States. The overall history of education in the United States can be chronicled as a story of the incremental expansion of access to schooling—first in the formation of the Latin grammar school, later through increased access to secondary schooling, and eventually through increased access to higher education. It is only natural that the earliest colleges in the colonies reflected the values of their European counterparts, particularly those of Oxford and Cambridge in Britain. Harvard College, the first university, established the British ideal of education for an elite and educated upper class, with a particular focus on the education of the clergy, when it opened in 1636 in Massachusetts. As the number of colleges grew—William and Mary in 1693, Yale in 1701, Princeton in 1746—the recognition of the value of these institutions for the preparation of professionals and a social elite steadily spread throughout the colonies.

Even though the curricula of various colleges differed somewhat, they shared the basic belief that college was only for a select few of those most likely to succeed. Although early in its history the United States would champion the idea of free public education, the structure and culture of the educational system was clearly designed to sort and select students. Surprisingly, no less a champion for general education than Thomas Jefferson (1782), the founder of the University of Virginia, proposed a system of three years of education for Virginia that ensured that only twenty boys of "best genius" in the state would be "raked from the rubbish annually" to receive up to ten years of schooling at public expense and that the university would ultimately admit only half of them each year.

While the establishment of state colleges and universities, such as the University of Georgia in 1785, the University of North Carolina in 1789, and the University of Tennessee in 1794, naturally expanded access to higher education, even greater impact came from another source—the growth of colleges and universities founded by various religious denominations. In 1776, only nine colleges existed within the colonies, but by the Civil War in 1861, the number had expanded to over two hundred and most were under the control of a religious denomination (Gutek, 1986). Although the curricula of the various colleges and universities gradually adjusted to reflect changing views of what students should be taught, the view that higher education was for the brightest and for the social elite remained intact.

The Morrill Acts of 1862 and 1890 granted public land along with a direct cash payment for the establishment and support of land-grant colleges in each state. This venture by the federal government once again increased the number of colleges and universities, but the acts also profoundly impacted thinking about the curricula of higher education. One of the requirements for receiving federal support through the Morrill Acts was that institutions provide instruction in agricultural and mechanical subjects, as well as in military training (Gutek, 1986).

In some ways, the establishment of the land-grant colleges and universities was a rebellion against the classical tenets of a liberal arts education, which more people began to see as unresponsive and irrelevant to the demands of an ever more complex and expanding agricultural and industrial society (Gutek, 1986). The Morrill Acts also influenced the diversity of students who enrolled in higher education. Eventually, seventeen Southern states established land-grant colleges for black Americans.

Access for All

The 20th century witnessed a dramatic increase in accessibility to college for Americans. In addition to landmark legal and societal shifts, such as desegregation and the Civil Rights Act of 1964, three separate forces shaped the dramatic rise in college attendance—the GI Bill, the establishment of junior and community colleges, and technology, the Internet, and online learning. Collectively, these initiatives permanently changed the landscape of higher education in America.

The GI Bill

It would be difficult to overestimate the impact of the GI Bill, not only on American society generally, but specifically on Americans' views of access to higher education. The GI Bill was passed soon after the end of the Second World War in response to fears that returning servicemen and -women would create high levels of unemployment, such as those experienced in the Great Depression. The bill itself was relatively simple. In short, the federal government promised to pay for college for any returning veteran who enrolled. The GI Bill dramatically increased the number of Americans who enrolled in college, from approximately 1.5 million in 1940 to almost 2.7 million at the end of the decade (Hunt, 2013). The impact on higher education was nothing short of astounding, not only in the numbers of veterans who enrolled in college, but in their characteristics.

It is not an overstatement to say that for the first time since the founding of the colonies, higher education opened up to average citizens. While the GI Bill is widely acclaimed as a vehicle for assisting returning veterans, the bill's greatest impact was in the change of mindset as to who could succeed in college. Not only did veterans enroll in large numbers, they performed very well, shattering the assumption that only sons—and to a limited degree, daughters—of the upper classes were college material. In 1947, the *New York Times* featured an article proclaiming, "Here is the most astonishing fact in the history of higher education. The G.I.'s are hogging the honor rolls and deans lists; they are walking away with the highest marks in all of their courses" (as quoted in Hunt, 2013, p. 1).

The Establishment of Junior and Community Colleges

The early 20th century saw the development of junior and community colleges as part of the higher education framework in America. The rationale for the establishment of two-year colleges beyond high school was multipurposed and has undergone periods of redefinition through the decades. Initially, the idea was to create colleges more suited to teach the curriculum of the traditional first two years of colleges—in other words, to push the first two years of undergraduate instruction out of the four-year college and university and to the new junior or community college.

By the middle of the 1920s, the curriculum of the community college expanded to meet the vocational and job-training needs of students. The Smith-Hughes Act of 1917, passed for the purpose of providing federal aid for vocational education, was a primary stimulus. Although the bill's most significant impact was on secondary schools, it also encouraged vocational and technical programs at many junior colleges (Gutek, 1986).

In the last half of the 20th century, community college systems dramatically expanded, leading to an increase in access to college. Virtually every state established a system of community colleges that not only provided vocational and technical preparation for a variety of fields but also served as a more affordable avenue for achieving a college degree—either an associate degree upon completion of a two-year course of study or ultimately a bachelor's degree from a four-year school upon completion of an additional two-year course of study.

Technology, the Internet, and Online Learning

It's been said that technology speeds things up. That has certainly been the case with access to higher education. Today's online courses and degree programs have their roots in the earliest correspondence courses of the mid- to late 1800s, many of which were specifically designed to expand educational access to women and working people. With the endorsement of such supporters as Cary Agassiz, founder of Radcliffe College, and William Rainey Harper, the first president of the University of Chicago, the development of correspondence courses gained momentum as a vehicle for citizens needing a convenient way to pursue additional training (Bower & Hardy, 2004).

By the 1920s, correspondence courses taught through the mail had begun to transition into distance education broadcast over more than two hundred radio stations, and by the 1950s, Western Reserve University was broadcasting the first televised classes. By the late 1980s, further developments in technology made possible live, two-way transmission of classes (Bower & Hardy, 2004). Fast-forward to the present, and blended courses, online courses, and the latest iteration—the massive open online course (MOOC)—are now central to the operation of most colleges and universities, both public and private.

Whether the motivation of traditional institutions was to achieve the loftier goal of expanding access to college or simply to compete with private, for-profit online colleges and universities offering a plethora of online courses and degrees, there is little doubt that the Internet has had a profound effect on access to higher education. According to the report *Going the Distance: Online Education in the United States, 2011* (Allen & Seaman, 2011), more than 6.1 million students took at least one online class during fall 2010—the ninth straight year for enrollment increases in online courses and a 10.1 percent increase over the previous year. Online courses and degree programs have become an important addition to the menu choices of postsecondary learners, but also a critical aspect of the long-term strategies of most colleges and universities.

However, as with previous movements that expanded access to higher education, faculty and administrators continue to debate the merits of doing so and the issue of maintaining high standards of quality. Several questions arise. Why do so many of the massive online courses begin with huge enrollments but have so few students who complete the courses? How do we deal with cheating in an online format? How do we provide effective student support in an environment that requires such a high degree of independence and self-motivation for success? Although the format of the courses may have changed, the challenge remains the same: ensuring a quality education to a progressively diverse student population within an increasingly competitive environment for higher education.

From Access to Success

The simple truth is this: there is a huge difference between attending college or university and graduating from college or university. As Vincent Tinto (2012) notes, even though access to college has more than doubled, from nearly nine million students in 1980 to nearly twenty million in 2011, overall, college completion rates have increased only slightly, if at all, with barely more than half of all four-year college students in the United States earning a bachelor's degree from their initial institution within six years. The dissatisfaction with low graduation rates has increased calls from state legislatures for higher education leaders to move beyond merely increasing student access. They seek instead a fundamental shift toward a focus on student success, specifically as defined by increased graduation rates.

Ironically, the roots of the current frustration with student success in higher education can be traced to America's concern with the state of K–12 education in the 1980s. Few could have predicted the impact that a national report critical of the state of K–12 education in the United States would ultimately have on higher education. In April of 1983, the National Commission on Excellence in Education issued its report *A Nation at Risk* and offered a grim assessment of K–12 public education in America. The opening paragraph was indicative of the report's depressing tone:

> Our nation is at risk. Our once unchallenged preeminence in commerce, industry, science, and technological innovation is being overtaken by competitors throughout the world. . . . The educational foundations of our society are presently being eroded by a rising tide of mediocrity that threatens our very future as a nation and as a people. . . . If an unfriendly foreign power had attempted to impose in America the mediocre educational performance that exists today, we might well have viewed it as an act of war. . . . We have, in effect, been committing an act of unthinking, unilateral educational disarmament. (p. 5)

A Nation at Risk launched a flurry of initiatives aimed at improving America's K–12 educational system. By 1986, more than three hundred state and national task forces had investigated the condition of public education. Efforts to improve achievement levels of students steadily continued through the 1990s, culminating in the much-publicized legislation of the George W. Bush administration, the No Child Left Behind Act of 2001. This standards-based education reform legislation was unique for a number of reasons, but perhaps the most compelling distinction was that underperforming schools and districts faced significant penalties.

With so much attention focused on K–12 public education, it was only a matter of time before calls began to ring out for improving America's system of public higher education. In 1993, *An American Imperative*, authored by the Johnson Foundation, outlined criticisms of higher education remarkably similar to the themes of *A Nation at Risk*, issued ten years previously. The introduction to *An American Imperative* included these lines:

> Like much of the rest of American education, the nation's colleges and universities appear to live by an unconscious educational rule of thumb that their function is to weed out, not to cultivate, students for whom they have accepted responsibility. . . . This hemorrhaging of our human resources occurs despite the low standards prevalent in American education and the existence of a wide diversity of institutions offering many options for students. It is almost as though educators take failure for granted. . . . Education is in trouble, and with it our nation's hopes for the future. (p. 1)

Since that time, Americans' frustration with their institutions has continued to build. While tuition costs soar, graduation rates remain flat. As they have historically, economic downturns spawn questions about the effectiveness of our educational system. Fueled by the financial crisis that began in 2007, fears that America might be losing its global economic competitiveness have renewed calls for greater accountability in higher education and generated a national discussion of what is frequently called "the college completion agenda."

In 2007, the College Board formed the Commission on Access, Admissions, and Success in Higher Education. Concerned with the number of students dropping out of the educational system along the K–16 pipeline, the commission established the goal of ensuring that 55 percent of Americans would hold a postsecondary degree by 2015. Two years later, in his first joint address to Congress, President Obama announced his goal of making the United States first in the world in the percentage of citizens holding a postsecondary degree or credential by the year 2020. The U.S. Department of Education pledged technical assistance and other resources in support of State College Completion Summits designed to promote strategies, policies, and action plans with the goal to significantly increase the number of Americans holding a postsecondary degree or certificate.

State legislatures, governors, private businesses, philanthropic organizations, and private trusts quickly rallied around the college completion agenda as the new goal for American higher education and the emerging benchmark for success. By June of 2013, thirty-three states had partnered with Complete College America (2014; http://completecollege.org), a nonprofit organization established in 2009 with the stated mission of working with states to "significantly increase the number of Americans with quality career certificates or college degrees and to close the attainment gaps for traditionally underrepresented populations."

Student Success—or Else!

Funded by organizations such as the Gates Foundation, the Lumina Foundation for Education, and the Carnegie Foundation, Complete College America urges states to take individual responsibility for setting state-specific college completion goals and to meet them by aggressively using state financial resources to create incentives for policies and action plans.

Tying state funding for higher education to defined benchmarks of student success has become a primary tactic of many college completion plans. For instance, in Tennessee, state-funded universities are no longer allocated money primarily based on enrollment. Instead, a three-year rolling average of improvement on such standards as the number of students crossing the twenty-four-, forty-eight-, or seventy-two-credit-hour threshold; the number of students per one hundred graduated; and overall graduation rates form the primary basis of a complex formula for the distribution of state funding.

Changes in state funding formulas signal a major shift in expectations for state colleges and universities—the public no longer considers it sufficient for them to merely accept students for admission. Universities are becoming accountable for supporting student learning and helping students successfully achieve a degree.

It is hard to disagree with either the practical need or the moral imperative to increase college success rates. Higher education represents a significant commitment of time and personal resources, as well as state and federal financial support. Four to six years of advanced education carry significant opportunity costs. Since only about 50 percent of students who enter a four-year institution graduate in six years, is it any wonder that students, their families, and state legislatures are demanding a better return on their investment?

Still, many observers of these trends are wary. They ask several important questions: Is this shift from access to completion possible without compromising the quality of undergraduate degrees? Will funding keep pace with the increased costs of providing the support necessary to assist a broader cross section of citizens in completing their degrees? Will universities sacrifice access and turn to enrolling only those students most likely to succeed because of their superior preparation and aptitude?

PLC as a Model for Cultural Change

Colleges and universities are not the first to raise these questions, as the same concerns were pervasive at the K–12 level at the beginning of the accountability movement. The very same questions gave rise to the PLC model: how to increase achievement without compromising the quality of the learning experience, how to sustain or increase access without sacrificing success, and how to provide enhanced academic support services in a time of limited funding. Successful primary and secondary schools of all types and sizes validate the energy, force, and influence of the PLC model. As noted, many businesses have successfully applied it as well.

Those same big ideas may now provide a useful framework for considering how best to create increased student success in higher education—but only in those institutions prepared to undertake a major cultural shift. The key concepts inherent in a professional learning community are, at their core, nothing less than a new way of approaching the work of a college or university. For some institutions, this requires a revolutionary change of perspective. Universities who take on the challenge of increasing student success—and who really mean it!—must focus relentlessly on student learning, work interdependently and with mutual accountability to ensure that students really do learn, and concentrate on data that either demonstrate that learning is occurring or show how learning can be improved.

The idea that we must refocus and reprioritize our efforts on student learning as the core function of a college or university is not new but remains controversial. In his book *Higher Learning*, Derek Bok (1986) asserts that despite the appearance of progress and great activity, institutions of higher education actually focus little of their effort on improving student learning. Acknowledging potential critics, he writes,

> Many educators will hotly dispute this assertion. After all, they will retort, what are deans and faculties doing when they revise the curriculum and develop new majors if not improving the quality of education? What are individual professors doing when they create new courses and labor to make old lectures better? This reaction is understandable. But the fact remains that the time faculties and administrators spend working together on education is devoted almost entirely to considering *what* their students should study rather than *how* they can learn more effectively or *whether* they are learning as much as they should. The professors who vote for new majors or

curricular reforms know very little about whether these
initiatives will actually help students progress toward the
educational goals of the institution. And rarely, if ever, do
they make a serious effort to find out. (p. 58)

How, then, can faculty, administrators, and staff lead their organizations toward the cultural shifts necessary to embrace a core
purpose of enhancing academic success and learning for all students?
Creating a new normal requires a determined, passionate, and persistent leadership; a clear understanding of the unique dynamics and
challenges within the academy; and a deep understanding of the
change processes required for systemic, organizational re-culturing.

Summary

The history of American public education can be chronicled,
in part, as an incremental journey toward increased access. Until
recently, the culture of public education—both in the K–12 arena
and especially in institutions of higher education—has been one of
"sorting and selecting" students, either by restricting who should
participate, or later, by allowing larger numbers of students in but
relatively few out. Until the 1990s, this culture of sorting and selecting has been seen as the natural order of education—a way to ensure
the cream rises to the top.

However, times have changed. Public expectations for higher
education have evolved from access for a few to increased access—
especially for groups of students who traditionally were underserved.
Increased access to public colleges and universities, coupled with a
rapid rise in tuition rates, has led to a corresponding call for significant increases in student retention and graduation rates. This
shift in expectations was initially reflected in the K–12 legislation,
the No Child Left Behind Act of 2001. The act called for puni-
tive consequences for schools with unacceptably high failure rates.
While No Child Left Behind focused on the K–12 arena, the focus
on increased student success began to affect public institutions of

higher education as well. The federal government, state legislatures, the NCAA, and taxpayers have begun to question the dismal graduation rates of public colleges and universities.

With increasing pressure focused on institutions of higher education, many university leaders are searching for effective ways to enhance student success rates—ways beyond simply raising admission requirements. Increasingly, the questions facing college and university leaders are, What can be done to increase retention and graduation rates of students who have traditionally been accepted for enrollment, and what structural and cultural changes can we make that will shift the focus from one of survival of the fittest to an emphasis on the success of each student—major by major, course by course, skill by skill? Fortunately, more is known than ever before about the most effective approaches to increasing student learning. The concepts and practices reflective of a high-performing professional learning community, if coupled with strong, passionate, and persistent leadership, are powerful, proven tools that can make the culture shifts necessary to enhance student success a reality.

CHAPTER 3

Leading Cultural Change

The decision to undertake change more often than not is accompanied by a kind of optimism and rosy view of the future that, temporarily at least, obscures the predictable turmoil ahead. But that turmoil cannot be avoided and how well it is coped with separates the boys from the men, the girls from the women. It is . . . rough stuff. . . . There are breakthroughs, but also brick walls.

—Seymour Sarason

There is no one right way to lead the cultural shifts necessary for a college or university to function as a true, high-performing professional learning community that strives to increase student academic success. Re-culturing any organization is difficult, and success depends on a number of factors—a sense of urgency, the availability of critical resources, the quality of personnel, the influence of organizational history, and so on—not to mention timing and sheer luck. However, the one indispensable factor necessary for success in any re-culturing effort is truly effective leadership. It is unreasonable to think that cultural change in any organization will simply bubble up from the bottom. One of the great ironies of organizational life is that the quality of bottom-up strategies and innovation depends on the quality of top-down direction and leadership (DuFour & Eaker, 1998).

The Leadership Context

One thing is absolutely certain. Culture shifts require strong, effective leadership at every level. There is no shortage of how-to-lead books in today's marketplace, and the ideas and suggestions found between the covers of these books are, for the most part, helpful for the leader who seeks to enhance his or her leadership toolkit. It certainly is possible to pick up an idea or two from these books or to reflect, "Well, I've never thought of that before," or "I've never thought of that in that way." However, the reader who is looking for the silver bullet—the one idea that will transform an organization—will likely be disappointed. This is because no two organizations are alike, and *this fact alone makes the leadership factor contextual.*

It is much more helpful to focus on proven, broad leadership concepts related to organizational development that are congruent with and support the practices of a PLC. Leading significant organizational change that will impact student success requires the development of a culture that is simultaneously loose and tight; an understanding of when top-down and bottom-up leadership styles are appropriate and effective; and a commitment to reciprocal accountability, to take action to close the knowing-doing gap, and to monitor and celebrate results.

A Simultaneously Loose and Tight Culture

Leaders of successful PLCs understand the power of creating a culture that is simultaneously loose (encouraging experimentation, autonomy, and creativity) and tight (nonnegotiable in such areas as the mission, vision, and core values). When Tom Peters and Robert Waterman (1982) studied some of America's best-run companies in order to determine what practices they had in common, they discovered the companies all have a culture that is both loose and tight. They observed that such a culture is, in essence, the coexistence of firm central direction and maximum individual autonomy: "Organizations that live by the loose-tight principle are on the one hand rigidly controlled, yet at the same time allow (indeed insist on) autonomy, entrepreneurship, and innovation from the rank and file" (Peters & Waterman, 1982, p. 318).

Waterman (1987), in *The Renewal Factor*, refers to this cultural characteristic somewhat differently. Waterman observes that organizations best be constantly "renewing" themselves, learning and adapting as times and circumstances change. He points out that renewing organizations treat everyone as a source of creative input. In describing companies that successfully renew themselves, he writes, "Their managers define the boundaries, and their people figure out the best way to do the job within those boundaries" (p. 7). Timothy Waters and Robert J. Marzano (2006) refer to the concept as "defined autonomy." Whatever the term, the importance for leaders who are seeking to re-culture their organization cannot be overemphasized.

Administrators, faculty, and staff who work collaboratively in a PLC constantly experiment, try new approaches, and make decisions, but all within the clearly defined framework of a collaboratively developed mission and vision, well-articulated values, and shared commitments. For the college or university functioning as a PLC, this framework builds on the previously described first big idea—that the core mission of the institution is to support learning for all students. While the institution supports a variety of other activities—research, service to the community, publication of new knowledge, development of new teaching methods, and so on—in a professional learning community, leaders must consistently ensure that these university activities do not eclipse the core mission to ensure student learning.

This aspect of leadership is particularly difficult for those who work within the college or university setting because higher education culture highly values individual autonomy. The simple fact is that those who resent *all* top-down direction and seek to work in a college or university with few, if any, boundaries for faculty and staff members will struggle in a PLC. They are likely to chafe against a culture that heavily emphasizes its institutional mission to enhance the academic success of students and that holds faculty and staff accountable to tangible measures of success to fulfill that mission.

Regardless of the written mission or vision of a college or university, a simple test to determine its core values is to ask the question, What trumps student learning and success? *Leaders of learning organizations face this test time and again.* When an idea that will benefit student learning conflicts with the happiness or autonomy (or both) of some members of faculty or staff, which do university leaders generally opt to satisfy? Too often, leaders choose the happiness of faculty and staff members over the good of students and the support of their learning. Skeptical? Consider this question: How do many academic departments determine course offerings and class schedules? In some cases—not all, but many—rather than focusing on creating schedules and times that reflect *student needs,* they often opt to build schedules around what the *faculty members desire.*

Creating a culture that is simultaneously loose and tight leads to a critical question—*tight about what?* The tightness of the culture is what makes the PLC framework so applicable to colleges and universities that believe it is within their mission—their core purpose—to move beyond a Darwinian, survival-of-the-fittest culture to one in which every student is given the time and assistance he or she needs to succeed. PLC colleges and universities collaboratively develop a clearly articulated mission and vision that define priorities, values, and commitments to support student success, and the leaders of these institutions promote, protect, defend, and celebrate the mission, vision, values, and commitments day in, day out, in every way possible.

Top-Down and Bottom-Up Leadership

There is an assumption, especially in institutions of higher education, that only *bottom-up* initiatives will be successful and that, therefore, they should implement only those initiatives that have originated from the faculty and staff and have broad consensus and support. But the complex journey of shifting from a culture of *access and content coverage* to one of *learning and graduation* is not likely to simply bubble up from the bottom. *While bottom-up leadership is necessary, by itself, it is rarely enough.* Successful cultural change requires high-quality, top-down leadership, direction, and support, especially in the beginning of the change process.

Let's face it—top-down leadership has gotten a bum rap. Some faculty members distrust virtually anything that comes from the upper level of administration. In some cases, the distrust comes from past conduct over time or singular events, or it simply may be fashionable to question authority at times. And certainly the prevailing wisdom is that improvement is simply not possible without the buy-in of those expected to implement the changes. DuFour (2007) summarizes this particular leadership dilemma in this way:

> Isn't it clear that improvement initiatives will not occur unless there is buy-in, a willingness of those engaged in the initiative to rally around it? Shouldn't the people closest to the action . . . decide the direction? But what happens when a well-intentioned leader does everything right in terms of engaging staff members in the consideration of a change initiative and makes a compelling case for moving forward, but the staff prefers the status quo? . . . Does professional autonomy extend to the freedom to disregard what is widely considered best practice in one's field? (p. 38)

It is perhaps a bit counterintuitive, but it takes strong and effective educational leaders to create truly empowered people throughout the organization (DuFour et al., 2010). Bottom-up ownership depends on highly effective top-down leadership. For these reasons, leaders must not wait to start the change process until the time is right, everyone is on board, or all the questions have been fully answered to everyone's satisfaction. Effective leaders never let their quest for perfection keep them from getting started. Sheryl Sandberg (2013a, 2013b), the CEO of Facebook and author of the best-selling book *Lean In*, says her favorite poster is by her desk and reads, "Done Is Better Than Perfect" (pp. 44–45). Focusing on enhancing student learning and success and engaging in the work of becoming a PLC should not be optional. The best time to begin is *right now*. If leaders wait until everyone is on board, the proverbial train will never leave the station.

As noted previously, this concept may particularly challenge those within the culture of a college or university who tend to carefully guard their professional autonomy, often seeing themselves more as independent contractors with greater affiliations to their academic disciplines than to the specific institutions that employ them. However, this very challenge reinforces the need for the top tiers of leadership to articulate with crystal clarity the core mission and hold all faculty and staff accountable. Leaders must be explicit about the priorities that guide their decision making and about the data that will demonstrate where the institution is and is not being effective in meeting those priorities.

Every professional within the institution bears a responsibility to put his or her best efforts toward meeting the stated goals. As DuFour (2007) argues,

> A professional is someone with expertise in a specialized field, an individual who has not only pursued advanced training to enter the field but who also is expected to remain current in its evolving knowledge base. A professional does not have the autonomy to ignore what is regarded as best practice in the field. (p. 42)

Leaders must be willing to use the power of their positions to ensure that faculty, particularly, apply the tenets of professionalism not only to the study of their own disciplines but also to their performance as educators within the classroom. Some may respond that once a faculty member receives tenure, leaders have no power to influence behavior. This observation is simply untrue. In most organizations, including universities, firing an employee is seldom the only recourse available to leaders. Effective leaders work tirelessly to create a culture in which most people, by far, want to do those things that will help students succeed. Shared commitments, collaborative teamwork, and a focus on the learning of each student provide leaders of a professional learning community with tools other than the threat of dismissal.

Reciprocal Accountability

Building the capacity for change and improvement requires more than assigning new responsibilities to people. Leaders have an obligation to provide faculty and staff members with the resources, training, mentoring, and support to help them successfully accomplish what leaders have asked them to do. Richard Elmore (2004) refers to this relationship as *reciprocal accountability*, explaining that "for every increment of performance I demand of you, I have an equal responsibility to provide you with the capacity to meet that expectation" (p. 93).

For example, successful university leaders who undertake significant cultural change use multiple channels to repeatedly explain *why* the shift and the initiatives that accompany it are important and what the benefits will be, especially in the long term. They consistently explain *why* undergoing basic cultural change is the *right thing to do*. And, most important, they don't do this just once or twice; it is a constant—drip, drip, drip.

Along with clearly explaining the *why*, effective leaders of change explicitly articulate *how* various initiatives and tasks connect. In multiple ways, they describe the big picture. But perhaps most important, they must communicate with strong *passion, excitement, energy, and a sense of resolve*. It is unlikely, within any organization, that anyone will be more motivated, more excited, or more passionate than the leaders. Appealing to rational thought alone will not be enough. If those in leadership positions cannot proclaim the moral and ethical imperative of helping students succeed and do it with passion and persistence, their well-intentioned efforts are doomed to failure. Increasing student retention rates in our universities requires leaders who can motivate and inspire faculty, staff, and students to achieve a clear and compelling purpose. Leaders cannot simply use the threat of budgetary pressures from state legislatures, for instance, to motivate faculty and staff members; it must come from a sense of ethical responsibility to admitted students whose tuition dollars the institution accepts. Leaders must not only advocate that changing is the right thing to do but also uphold the right reasons for doing it.

Reciprocal accountability also requires a clear explanation and description of the *what*—exactly what leaders expect of various individuals, colleges, departments, and groups and what the work should look like when completed. Most of us can remember being part of a committee assigned a task without clear direction or explanation. As frustration sets in, someone always asks, "Well, what exactly are we supposed to do?" Unless those in leadership positions have a clear conceptual framework for the work that individuals need to do and the ability to clearly articulate directions and expectations, confusion and frustration will reign and well-intended efforts will bog down.

Those who are asked to undertake initiatives and assignments, such as those designed to increase student retention, also deserve some suggestions as to *how* they might successfully do their work. In a professional *learning* community (and we are emphasizing the word *learning* purposefully), the first step is always to gain shared knowledge through collective inquiry—seeking knowledge of best practices to learn from the work of others. It's difficult to overstate the importance of this high-performing PLC characteristic. Ironically, for institutions of higher education, this, in and of itself, represents a significant cultural shift. One would think if any institution would automatically seek the best information about a topic or issue when making plans or solving problems, it would be institutions of higher education. Yet, groups charged with developing plans or initiatives often end up merely averaging the opinions of those within the group. Unfortunately, in many colleges and universities, this is the norm, and seeking best practice is the exception.

For example, when colleges and universities set out on the journey to significantly increase student completion rates, it seems logical to first learn what the most successful colleges are already doing. While no institution should blindly adopt the practices of others, in a PLC culture, the first step is always to seek best practice—the best of what is already known—much like in other professions, such as medicine or law. Those in leadership positions are responsible for making process suggestions that will help every group think about how they might successfully complete their assigned tasks.

Of course, clearly articulating a time frame for planning, projects, or new initiatives enhances the likelihood of success for everyone. This point seems obvious, yet it is often overlooked. Significant initiatives involving the work of multiple groups require a clearly articulated calendar of when they must complete various tasks. Not only does this let groups know when they are due to complete their work, but by clearly communicating why a particular due date is critical in relation to what others are doing, everyone gets a sense that the overall plan is well thought out. This increases the confidence level throughout the organization.

Linked closely with articulating what individuals and groups are asked to do is the issue of resource allocation. When thinking of reciprocal accountability, one of the first things that should come to mind is providing the resources that groups need to be successful. Timely and appropriate resource allocation is critically important. Individuals and groups cannot successfully complete assigned tasks without the appropriate training, materials, and other required resources. Appropriate examples can be a particularly helpful resource. High-quality examples can go a long way to speed up the work, but they can also serve as guides to what the project should look like when completed, cutting down on the need for significant editing and redoing of tasks.

One often overlooked aspect of reciprocal accountability is the need for periodic feedback, which should be provided during the work, rather than exclusively upon completion. Everyone deserves to know if he or she is on the right track and if the work he or she is producing is meeting expectations. Feedback along the way reduces anxiety, since all those involved will have confidence in the fact that what they are doing and how they are doing it are correct.

The Knowing-Doing Gap

The ultimate challenge for leaders is not only knowing what to do, but acting effectively on that knowledge. While this may seem obvious, Pfeffer and Sutton (2000) in *The Knowing-Doing Gap* contend that the lack of knowledge is seldom the reason organizations don't do what they need to do. Instead, they fail to meet their stated goals because of an inability or unwillingness to implement the knowledge they already have. Peter Block (2002) in *The Answer to How Is Yes: Acting on What Matters* points out, "We deny ourselves action when we keep looking for more and more information to ensure greater certainty as a condition for moving on" (p. 42).

What does this mean within the context of leading cultural change in universities to significantly and systemically impact student success? Simply this: leaders at all levels must possess an action orientation. They must not wait for universal agreement. Leaders will never convince everyone that the university must support and assist students in their academic pursuits. The challenge for leaders is to first change people's behavior; over time, as evidence emerges of more student success, minds will change.

Leaders don't wait to establish a culture of trust or until they have learned the answers to everything they will need to know. Rather, they get started, and then they get better—never letting the quest for perfection keep them from beginning at all. The belief that drives those who effectively lead cultural change is this: "We must first gain shared knowledge and get started—then continually get better!" Mastering the art of getting started and then getting better is a prerequisite for developing a research-based, data-driven culture of continuous improvement.

Progress and the Celebration of Results

Leaders monitor; they constantly check on what they value the most. It does little good to speak eloquently and passionately about the importance of improving student success and not regularly monitor the impacts of these efforts. This is perhaps the most significant way leaders communicate institutional values. Phrases that become clichés do so for a reason—because they contain a strong element of truth. The cliché "What gets monitored gets done!" is an excellent example.

This cultural shift from a focus on intentions (constantly planning for improved results) to a culture of improved results (determining if more students successfully matriculate from course to course, year to year) is a fundamental characteristic of a PLC. It is important that members of the organization monitor student success frequently, in multiple ways, and collaboratively analyze the resulting data to form the basis for ongoing decision making and operating adjustments.

Just as highly effective instructors monitor the learning of individual students on a frequent and timely basis, providing them with feedback and encouragement to get better, effective leaders do the same with individuals and groups as they work on strategic initiatives. It is highly ineffective to monitor progress only on an annual basis. People need regular feedback, encouragement, and support if they are to improve. Effective leaders realize it does little good to simply monitor results at the end; improvement comes when they use data to provide feedback, support, and encouragement. Simply using monitoring practices to apply pressure is, by itself, ineffective. They must gracefully apply relentless pressure (Eaker & Keating, 2012).

Not only do effective leaders monitor results on a formative, ongoing basis, but they do so by collaboratively analyzing multiple forms of data, from multiple sources. Working closely with those responsible for creating change and implementing new initiatives, they review both quantitative and qualitative data and monitor the quality of products that individuals and groups produce. Together, senior leadership, faculty, and other staff must look for patterns of data and understand that these patterns may be much more important than the results from an isolated event. Patterns, once identified, can be used to fine-tune plans and initiatives or, when necessary, to make the decision to abandon those activities that are not showing positive impact.

Frequently monitoring progress is not the only way leaders shape organizational culture. Equally imperative is the frequent and meaningful recognition and celebration of results along the way. An important challenge for leaders who hope to change organizational culture and thus improve results is to motivate faculty and staff to continually improve when the journey, by its very nature, has no end. The solution is clear: create small wins and celebrate results (DuFour et al., 2008). In the absence of recognition and celebration, organizational values lose their meaning. People will simply not believe we care deeply about the things we advocate if we fail to monitor, report, and celebrate progress (Deal & Kennedy, 1982). John Kotter and Dan Cohen (2002) concur: "What we don't know is not a win" (p. 129).

Recognizing and celebrating the small victories along the way is also the right thing to do. One of the most frequent complaints from people across all levels within organizations is that their efforts go unappreciated (Patterson, Grenny, Maxfield, McMillan, & Switzler, 2008). Administrators, faculty, and staff want recognition for the results of their efforts. The power of public recognition and celebration of achievements that tie directly to organizational values and goals is truly astonishing. Equally astounding is the degree of demoralization that results from the lack of recognition and celebration. Effective leaders go beyond recognizing this fact; they act!

Summary

There is no one right way to lead the cultural changes necessary to enhance student success. However, there is one indispensable prerequisite—strong, effective leadership. Universities that attempt to improve student retention must recognize that in the absence of effective leadership throughout the university—especially at the top levels—faculty and staff will not know what to do, why they should do it, or even if their efforts really matter.

Universities seeking to improve student success must strive to find the correct balance between being tight about the university mission, vision, and values, on the one hand, and being loose about how to get there on the other. They must balance top-down and bottom-up leadership and provide administrators, faculty, and staff with the resources they need to accomplish what is asked of them. Leaders must be relentlessly insistent on closing the gap between what they know and what they do. Finally, they must constantly shape the culture of the university by frequently monitoring results and by recognizing and celebrating accomplishments along the way. In short, the ultimate effectiveness of every initiative to improve student success will depend on the effectiveness of leaders throughout the university.

CHAPTER 4

Enhancing Student Success Through a Commitments-Driven University

Terms travel easily . . . but the underlying concepts do not.

—Michael Fullan

Organizations on the journey of continuous improvement very often begin by undertaking a re-examination of mission, vision, and values. The aim of such a review—to build a broadly shared foundation in support of goal setting for the future—is admirable. However, it is easy for institutions to become mired in this stage of review and spend months, and sometimes years, wordsmithing long, carefully crafted mission and vision statements in the hope that the right document creates the conditions necessary to deliver improvements and desired outcomes.

The most effective leaders do more than simply revisit or recraft existing mission and vision statements to truly impact student success, especially retention and graduation rates. Effective leaders of deep, systemic organizational change view the building of these shared foundations as a chance to issue a significant call to action. They never mistake writing a mission statement for getting things done. They understand that the crucial ingredients for creating change are leadership, passion, and the will to act.

Rather than using the tired, traditional jargon of *mission* and *vision*, effective university leaders engage the entire organization in a deep, rich, and meaningful examination of four fundamental questions of institutional commitment: (1) *Why* do we exist—what is our core purpose? (2) *What* must our organization become if we are to achieve our core purpose? (3) *How* must we behave—what commitments are we willing to make in order to become the organization we seek to become? and (4) *How will we mark our progress* (DuFour et al., 2010)?

Articulating a Clear and Compelling Purpose

It seems logical that undertaking the cultural shifts that will lead to significant institutional improvement would first focus on the two questions, What are we going to do? and How are we going to do it? Not so! Researchers, writers, and organizational theorists contend, instead, the place to start with is the *why*. We must begin by articulating the clear and compelling *purpose* of the organization.

The first question any organization must address if it hopes to improve results is that of purpose (Drucker, 1992). Leaders can only align expectations and behavior throughout the organization when they are clear about the organization's core purpose—what it stands for and what it hopes to become. James Collins and Jerry Porras (1997) observe, "Contrary to popular wisdom, the proper first response to a changing world is NOT to ask, 'How should we change,' but rather, 'What do we stand for and why do we exist?'" (p. xiv). In *Start With Why*, Simon Sinek (2009) contends that "knowing your WHY is not the only way to be successful, but it is the only way to maintain a lasting success and have a greater blend of innovation and flexibility" (p. 50).

However, it's not enough to broadly communicate the organization's core purpose (mission) and its view of the future (vision). It is critical that these building blocks of organizational culture be both *clear* and *compelling*. Leaders must win both the hearts and the minds of the members of the organization and of the people they hope to serve.

Communicating a Clear Message of Enhancing Student Success

Mike Schmoker (2004b) notes, "Clarity precedes competence" (p. 85). While universities are called on to focus on multiple goals, the core purpose of any institution of higher education must ultimately be learning—whether it's classroom instruction, research, or assisting others to learn through service. Therefore, university leaders must *clearly* articulate the institution's core purpose of supporting others in their learning and helping them succeed to everyone, including faculty, staff, students, and the larger community. As noted previously, a focus on learning is a distinctive departure from the traditional university focus on teaching or on sorting out the less elite students.

It's particularly critical that university leaders at every level clearly communicate that a central tenet of the university's mission is to *support students in their efforts to succeed year by year to graduation and that every office, at every level, and in every division of the university has a role to play.* Simply declaring that the university must and will improve student success will prove woefully inadequate. The graduation rate is a critical measure of success. Students may experience measures of success in some classrooms or may remain enrolled through scores of credit hours. But if they don't cross the finish line at graduation, they will not reap the benefits of a completed college degree—and a number will bear significant debt. The public increasingly judges universities on this very measurable indicator of success.

The message of supporting student success as evidenced by timely graduation must be *frequently* communicated, at every opportunity.

Effective communication is simple and succinct, and a few compelling ideas drive it. Leaders must repeat, emphasize, and contextualize the clear message of the *why* as often as possible. Administrators, faculty, and staff commonly see individual tasks and activities as a relentless stream of "just one thing after another" and do not recognize the overall connection to a larger whole. It is the leader's responsibility to make sure these connections are clear. The leader must be able to succinctly answer the question of why the institution exists with the simple answer: "Our core purpose is to support student learning and to help students successfully graduate from this institution!"

Conveying a Compelling Purpose

It's not enough that leaders clearly and frequently communicate the *why* message. The message—the core purpose—must also be *compelling*, causing people to want to act and to fully participate in achieving a worthwhile purpose. Most administrators, faculty, and staff are willing to work hard and even go above and beyond typical expectations *if* they believe the purpose is worthwhile.

Inspiring others to act is linked directly to the ability of leaders to articulate, time and again, a compelling purpose—not just any purpose, not even just a clear purpose, but a *compelling* purpose—that calls the institutional community to action.

By clearly conveying a compelling purpose throughout the institution and in multiple ways, leaders can begin to influence others to act—to behave differently. Sinek (2009) emphasizes how clearly communicating a compelling *why* can serve as a powerful inspiration for others to act. He points to Martin Luther King Jr.'s 1963 "I Have a Dream" speech during the march on Washington as a powerful example:

> Dr. King was absolute in his conviction. He *knew* change had to happen in America. His clarity of WHY, his sense of purpose, gave him the strength and energy to continue his fight against often seemingly insurmountable

odds . . . and that speech was about what he believed,
not how they were going to do it. He gave the "I Have
a Dream" speech, not the "I Have a Plan" speech. . . . It
wasn't the details of his plans that earned him the right
to lead. It was what he believed and his ability to communicate it clearly that people followed. (pp. 126–129)

In the absence of inspiration, leaders are left with few options
other than manipulating the behavior of others through a combination of sticks and carrots. Sinek (2009) notes, "There are only two
ways to influence human behavior; you can manipulate it or you
can inspire it" (p. 17). Of course, manipulation is common in virtually all organizations. Manipulations include such tactics as threats
and the creation of fear (the stick) or, conversely, the promise of a
reward, such as a promotion or a raise (the carrot). While manipulation is common in most organizations, it is usually inadequate by
itself to create deep cultural change.

For example, as an increasing number of state legislatures tie university funding to student retention and graduation rates, some
university leaders hold up the potential negative effects of a lack of
funding—loss of jobs, elimination of programs, or cuts in services—
as the primary reason for improving student success rates. While
these messages may certainly reflect reality, such fear tactics are not
likely to prove effective in changing the attitudes, behaviors, and
commitments of enough people and to a sufficient degree to create
significant change. The fact is that under the conditions we have
described, most people convince themselves that while others may
be negatively impacted, they will not personally be affected by any
loss of funding. Given the recent history of funding issues in higher
education, many will further believe that even if budget cuts take
place, tuition increases will offset any loss in funding.

Rather than turning to fear tactics, the primary message of leaders should instead be inspirational; universities should focus on
enhancing student success because it's the *right* thing—rather than

the *must* thing—to do. The institution has an ethical obligation to help students succeed both academically and in nonacademic areas of university life. Everyone in every division, every office, and every program should strive to create a university that he or she would want his or her own son or daughter to attend, and for most people, that means forging creative and effective ways to help students when they struggle and to enhance and enrich their learning when they succeed. (As a side note, the question of whether or not the faculty and staff want their own children to attend the college or university where they are employed can be a very telling barometer of institutional culture and effectiveness.) In short, members of the institution should create a culture of support and caring because it's what they *should* do—what they would want for their own sons and daughters—not because it is *required*!

Connecting Purpose With Action

A word of caution is in order. Clearly, frequently, and consistently articulating the university's core purpose or even rewriting the university's mission statement is not the same as actually taking action. There is an enormous difference between *rewriting* a mission statement and actually *living* the mission. While the process of making the enhancement of student success a key aspect of a university's core purpose must begin with an emphasis on the *why*, it will only have an impact when it is moved quickly and visibly to the *do*. Mistaking a mission for action is a recipe for failure. Pfeffer and Sutton (2000) find that ineffective organizations often equate writing a mission statement with actually bringing the mission statement to life. In fact, they could find no correlation between simply writing a mission statement and how people within organizations act.

The challenge for university leaders is to articulate and embed in the policies, practices, and procedures of the institution the moral purpose of helping students succeed. It must be done at every level and in such a way that everyone questions their existing attitudes, commitments, and behaviors and aligns them with that core purpose. The key to effective communication is to align what one says and what one does. Leaders need not be eloquent in their communications, but they must demonstrate consistency between what they say and what they do—day in, day out (DuFour et al., 2010). Kotter (1996) concurs, noting, "When leaders' actions are inconsistent with what they contend are their priorities, those actions overwhelm all other forms of communication" (p. 36).

Nowhere is this alignment more important than in two specific issues: what university leaders check on—that is, what they pay attention to—and what they frequently and meaningfully celebrate and reward. Administrators, faculty, and staff will pay much more attention to what their leaders monitor, evaluate, and reward than to their pronouncements.

What does all of this have to do with enhancing student success and improving retention and graduation rates? In a word, *everything*! Unless university leaders clearly articulate—over and over—a compelling reason why the university focuses on enhancing student success, their efforts will be no more than feeble attempts to manipulate the culture around the edges, the net result marginal at best. University leaders must ask themselves, "What behaviors—what actions—on my part, as well as those within my area of responsibility, will best communicate daily that we are actively committed to the university's purpose of supporting student success and graduation?" Equally important, every leader within the university must reflect on his or her basic assumptions and management style and ask, "Am I inadvertently or even purposefully communicating—through my actions or the actions of those whom I supervise—a message that is incongruent with a mission of enhancing student success?"

Developing a Shared Vision of the Future

Despite its importance, clearly articulating a compelling core purpose for the university still isn't sufficient to create the necessary cultural change. Terms such as *improving retention rates* or *enhanced student success* travel easily, but the university can only realize the underlying concepts—the ideals—when everyone within it clearly understands the implications of the terms. Building a solid foundation for cultural change in any organization requires that leaders also focus their efforts on forming a clear vision of what supporting student success will look like and how the future will be significantly better than the current reality. In other words, university leaders must create a recognizable target that beckons, with both meaning and clear implications for behavior.

In 1985, Warren Bennis and Burt Nanus published their groundbreaking study of effective leadership behavior. Their book, *Leaders: The Strategies for Taking Charge,* is the result of a combination of interviews and observations with ninety of America's top leaders from both the corporate and public service sectors (Bennis & Nanus, 1985). They synthesized their findings into four overarching strategies, with the very first strategy being "attention through vision." They write,

> Management of attention through *vision* is the *creation of focus.* All ninety people interviewed had an *agenda,* an unparalleled concern with outcome. Leaders are the most results-oriented individuals in the world, and results get attention. Their visions or intentions are compelling and pull people toward them. Intensity coupled with commitment is magnetic. And these intense personalities do not have to coerce people to pay attention; they are so intent on what they are doing that, like a child completely absorbed with creating a sand castle in a sandbox, they draw others in. (p. 28)

A widely shared, compelling vision of the future not only inspires others to act; it also provides a blueprint for how to get from point A to point B.

Again, Martin Luther King Jr.'s "I Have a Dream" speech (1963) is an excellent example of connecting an overarching, compelling purpose to a vision of the future. King did much more than proclaim that he had a dream; he continued in his speech to describe his dream—his vision for the United States. People continue to quote and replay his speech, and it still beckons to them in a powerful way.

King (1963) connected his dream—his vision of the future—to a call for action. He urged those in attendance,

> Go back to Mississippi, go back to Alabama, go back to South Carolina, go back to Georgia, go back to Louisiana, go back to the slums and ghettos of our Northern cities, knowing that somehow this situation can and will be changed.

One of the most difficult challenges university leaders face when creating a culture focused on student learning and success is that of envisioning this new target—the task of painting a vivid portrait of a different kind of institution of higher education. Leading cultural change in any organization—but particularly in a college or university—isn't for the faint of heart. However, the title of *leader* does carry with it certain expectations. Leaders in higher education must expect to encounter both active and passive resistance when challenging the fundamental tenets of a deeply ingrained culture.

The effective university leader constantly and consistently conveys a message of moving beyond merely teaching—just covering the course content and letting the chips fall where they may—to supporting students in their learning. There is obviously a great deal of difference between what is taught and what is learned. A leader would not build a vision of student success on the belief "It's my job to teach, but it's the students' job to learn." Instead, an effective leader bases the new vision on the belief that the university has a responsibility to provide support, encouragement, and resources to help every admitted student meet his or her full potential. And they must do so with the clear understanding that students learn at different paces and in different ways.

From Communicating to Believing

Developing an engaging target that beckons toward a new future does not happen quickly or in a single round of newsletters, open forums, or staff meetings. Leaders must communicate this vision time and again and in multiple formats. More important, leaders must do so in ways that cause others to believe in and adopt the vision as their own. Virtually all universities distribute their mission and vision statements throughout multiple forms of university print material, as well as multimedia formats. Marketing the university brand has become a full-time, highly sophisticated enterprise. However, the public has become more sophisticated too, and leaders must move beyond marketing and branding if they are to successfully convince prospective students and their parents that university personnel, in every division and at all levels, will support them in their college career. Successfully communicating the target so that it has an impact requires, at a minimum, two elements: examples of how the university puts the vision into action and evidence of success.

Here's an example. Most university athletic departments do an excellent job of providing both examples and evidence of their success to both internal and external audiences. When recruiting prospective athletes, for instance, a key selling point they emphasize is how the university supports student athletes in their academic pursuits. When recruits and their parents visit the campus, they hear about academic counselors to track each athlete's academic performance, tutoring programs, and online academic help, and they often visit a modern facility dedicated to the academic support of student athletes. The important point is that the coaches can describe specific programs and resources in place to support student success. And they can also provide data that demonstrate the successful outcomes that the support creates. Every athletic department in Division I can point to its NCAA graduation rate compared to other universities. These program examples, coupled with data, go a long way to convince others that the university, particularly the athletic department, takes supporting student athletes' academic success seriously—and that they are good at it.

Benefits of a Clear and Compelling Vision of the Future

It would be difficult to overemphasize the importance of effectively and vividly describing the future that leaders seek for their organizations. Bennis and Nanus (1985) write,

> If there is a spark of genius in the leadership function at all, it must lie in this transcending ability, a kind of magic, to assemble—out of all the variety of images, signals, forecasts and alternatives—a clearly articulated vision of the future that is at once simple, easily understood, clearly desirable, and energizing. (p. 103)

Such a vision can be enormously beneficial to both the university and its students—if it gives focus to the right things in the right ways.

DuFour et al. (2008) point out that there are a number of important benefits to a clear and compelling vision. A clear vision can provide meaning for people's work and can increase the commitment they have for the work they are being asked to do. A shared vision also creates a proactive orientation—shifting from reaction after the fact to action ahead of time to staying ahead of the curve. A vision of the future gives direction to people throughout the organization. This helps all those involved understand how their roles fit into a larger purpose. Such clarity simplifies the decision-making process and empowers people to act with increased confidence. Another benefit is that a clear vision can help establish specific standards of excellence. Perhaps most important, a clear and compelling vision, when constantly and consistently communicated in multiple ways, creates a clear agenda for action. It is impossible for a university, or any organization, to make significant and systemic improvements unless it has clarified what it seeks to become.

The Standard

When thinking of how well their organization communicates its vision, leaders should ask themselves a number of important questions. Kotter (1996) suggests asking if the vision is imaginable, desirable, feasible, focused, and communicable. DuFour et al. (2008) are even more succinct. They recommend asking the following questions.

1. Does the vision result in people throughout the organization acting in new ways that are aligned with the intended direction that has been established?

2. Do people at all levels use the vision to guide their day-to-day decisions?

3. Is the vision explicitly used to modify structures, processes, and procedures to better align with the intended direction? (pp. 142–143)

Effectively clarifying the vision of an institution requires finding a way to give real-world meaning to the target. The best strategy is to bring the target to a personal level for each member of the organization, using the following questions to guide decision making, planning, and budgeting in all areas of the institution.

- What would the university look like if the leaders in every division and every office really meant it when they said they would encourage and support students in their academic and nonacademic pursuits? If an undercover television news team spent two weeks on our campus, what would they see people actually doing to enhance student success?

- What kind of encouragement, assistance, and support would we want for our own sons or daughters if they attended this college? Are we striving to create a university culture in which we would want our own sons or daughters to learn or a culture in which adults would like to work independently and autonomously? Do we place a higher priority on student learning or on the happiness of the administrators, faculty, and staff who work for the university?

Ultimately, to be effective, a vision of the future must touch the emotions of administrators, faculty, staff, students, parents, and the larger community. To invite focus on the function of institutions, leaders must establish and declare a vision of what those institutions are. But a vision is much more than a simple goal statement printed in hiring and marketing materials. Bennis and Nanus (1985) remind us:

> A vision cannot be established in an organization by edict, or by the exercise of power or coercion. It is more an act of persuasion, of creating an enthusiastic and dedicated commitment to a vision because it is right for the times, right for the organization, and right for the people who are working in it. (p. 107)

Harnessing the Power of Shared Values and Commitments

University leaders who undertake the cultural shifts necessary to improve student success, who do so for the right reasons, and who articulate a clear and compelling vision of the future must then realize that to be successful, they need to harness the power of developing shared values and commitments. It is in its values that an organization finds its meaning, and it is through the shared commitments that everyone prepares to move the organization to action.

By emphasizing a positive vision of the future that articulates the university's commitment to enhancing student success, university leaders can create a sense of optimism and focus. Simultaneously, such a vision generates a critically important new question: What are the beliefs, attitudes, and behaviors that personnel throughout the university must exhibit to realize the vision of enhancing student success? In other words, what values must the university promote, protect, defend, and celebrate as it moves toward the university it seeks to become (DuFour & Eaker, 1998)?

Shared values serve the important purpose of bringing together diverse individuals with different backgrounds, beliefs, and agendas. James Kouzes and Barry Posner (2007) emphasize this point in *The Leadership Challenge*:

> Although credible leaders honor the diversity of their many constituencies, they also stress their common values. Leaders build on agreement. They don't try to get everyone to be in accord on everything—this goal is unrealistic, perhaps even impossible. Moreover, to achieve it would negate the very advantages of diversity. But to take a first step, and then a second, and then a third, people must have some common core of understanding. After all, if there's no agreement about values, then what exactly is the leader—and everyone else—going to model? If disagreements over fundamental values continue, the result is intense conflict, false expectations, and diminished capacity. (p. 60)

If university leaders are to be successful in their efforts to improve student success as measured by retention and graduation rates, they must be able to build and affirm a set of shared values focused on supporting and encouraging students in both the academic and nonacademic aspects of their college experience.

At first glance, developing these shared values—what the university stands for—may seem relatively easy. In fact, it is very difficult and requires patience and skill. What makes the development of shared values and commitments so difficult is the emphasis that leaders must place on the *shared* aspect of value development. Kouzes and Posner (2007) remind us:

> For values to be truly shared, they must be more than advertising slogans. They must be deeply supported and broadly endorsed beliefs about what's important to the

people who hold them. Constituents must be able to enumerate the values and must have common interpretations of how those values will be put into practice. They must know how the values influence their own jobs and how they directly contribute to organizational success. (p. 67)

Developing a sense of shared values is particularly difficult in organizations like universities, which have a long history and tradition of individualism and autonomy among the faculty and between distinctive colleges, schools, and departments. Yet, embracing this challenge is what being a leader is all about. Change isn't easy, and by its very definition, being effective requires leaders to take on the hard work of leading.

How can university leaders move beyond reliance on mere advertising slogans and effectively communicate those values the university holds dear? They must understand that how they act— what they do, rather than what they say—communicates their values. DuFour and Eaker (1998) point out that people learn what their organizations truly value by observing and answering the following questions.

- What do leaders spend their time *planning* for?
- What behaviors do leaders *model*?
- What do leaders *monitor*? What do they frequently check on?
- What behaviors are leaders willing to *confront*?
- What do leaders *celebrate*?
- What *questions* are leaders attempting to answer?
- On what basis do leaders allocate *resources*?

Leaders must understand that determining the answers to these questions, collectively, is how people throughout the organization learn what matters most. University leaders who are verbally committed to enhancing student success must ask themselves, "What values do I really promote through my behavior? Is there congruence between what I do and what I say?"

While organizational values that leaders widely communicate make it clear to everyone how they should act, broadly shared commitments to those values ultimately drive genuine cultural change. If leaders truly believe the values, then what are they prepared to do, what commitments are those in leadership positions prepared to make in order for the university to become what they have said they seek for it to become? The engine that drives cultural change is shared commitments, collaboratively developed and articulated in every division and at every level.

The power of shared commitments lies in their impact on behavior, and as Kotter and Cohen (2002) remind us, the challenge of changing organizational culture is "changing people's behavior" (p. 2). If university leaders want to make a significant impact on student success rates, they must focus on aligning behavior throughout the university with its core values, and the first step in doing so is to clearly articulate the commitments that people are willing to make at every level within the university.

It is helpful to think of shared commitments as a series of *if-then* statements. For example, *if* leaders want more students to experience academic success, *then* they must identify those courses with significantly high failure rates and provide students in those courses with additional support. It is the leader's job to use every available strategy and best practice to help members of the organization identify those commitments that they must and will make in order to become a university where all students receive the support necessary to meet their maximum potential.

Of course, the presence of clearly articulated commitments does not necessarily inspire every person within the university to live by them on a daily basis. Discrepancies between what people say and do continue to exist in every organization. Mutual accountability and peer pressure do not always prevail, and in those cases, leaders must be willing to address the problem.

Robert Eaker and Janel Keating (2008) refer to this as closing the "expectations-acceptance gap" (p. 16). Richard DuFour (2007) notes,

> If educational leaders contend that the purpose of the organization is to ensure that all students learn at high levels (as virtually all of our mission statements contend) and then they allow people throughout the organization to opt out of practices and processes that are clearly more effective at promoting learning than the prevailing practices, they send mixed messages that will succeed in creating confusion and cynicism but will fail to improve. . . . Thus they will fail as leaders. (p. 41)

The presence of *collective* commitments casts university leaders in a new role in relation to the people who report to them—as promoters and protectors of the vision and of the collective pledges of people to make that vision a reality. When leaders hold people accountable for the collective commitments of the group, they operate with the full moral authority of the group behind them, rather than a simple "I'm the boss" framework.

Summary

The change necessary to create cultural shifts that result in increased student success is complex and incremental, and leading it is difficult. Effective leaders undertake this journey by building a strong foundation with the mission, articulating a core purpose that addresses the question of *why*, and creating a clear and compelling vision of the future that shows exactly what it will look like. They shape behavior throughout the organization by promoting, protecting, and defending a collaboratively developed set of organizational values and commitments that align with the organization's mission and vision of the future—answering the question of *how*. Leaders who bypass this step or who address these questions only superficially are likely to find that their future efforts to change organizational culture—and behavior—have a marginal impact, at best.

CHAPTER 5

Capturing the Power of Collaborative Teaming

Interdependence is what organizations are all about. Productivity, performance, and innovation result from joint action, not just individual efforts and behavior.

—Jeffery Pfeffer and Robert Sutton

If university leaders really mean it (and this is a huge *if*) when they proclaim that enhancing student success is the core of their mission, they must realize that they can only successfully accomplish this in significant and systemic ways within a collaborative culture. Traditional assumptions about and approaches to collaboration in most universities make their attempts woefully inadequate. To make a significant impact on student success, university leaders must break free from the traditional isolation of most institutions of higher education and instead rely on high-performing *collaborative teams* as the organizing principle and cultural norm.

A significant disconnect exists between the generally accepted belief that meaningful collaboration is (or *should* be) normal and the actual day-to-day *reality* of individual isolation. This is especially true in the culture of most large public universities. Peter Magolda (2005) observes, "The extreme ideal of egalitarian exchange, while an espoused model for collaboration, is unlikely to represent an enacted model for collaboration" (p. 19). Most people, including university employees, believe that universities function as highly collaborative cultures. Yet, close examination reveals a strikingly different reality.

The cultural history of higher education stems, for the most part, from a tradition in which individual faculty members teach classes, pursue research and other scholarly endeavors, and participate in some measure of campus or public service. By and large, the university rewards faculty members with tenure and promotion for discipline-based, scholarly work arising from their independent research agendas. They rarely receive rewards for their contributions to broader university goals. While they may consider collaboration worthwhile in the abstract, it has not been, historically, an integral part of the university reward structure.

This culture of autonomous goal setting and independent planning and prioritization is not limited to the academic areas of colleges and universities. Academic affairs, student affairs, business affairs, alumni affairs, athletics, and other divisions and departments also work largely in isolation and, in some instances, even compete with one another.

This is not to say that these silos of isolation are limited to institutions of higher education. Operational silos and departmental independence are the norm in many large organizations, almost always with a detrimental effect on collective goal attainment. The idea that protecting one's turf and internal competition are healthy motivators has impeded the effectiveness of both individuals and organizations.

How can one explain the fact that universities, of all places, generally do such a poor job of developing strong collaborative cultures? A lack of a clear understanding or agreement about what effective collaboration is—and equally important, what it isn't—contributes to a culture of *collaboration-lite* in many institutions of higher education.

What Collaboration Is (and Is Not)

There are a variety of interpersonal and even interdepartmental relationships in the workplace that may masquerade as being collaborative. For example, a workplace culture in which people frequently communicate with each other and therefore appear to get along may be mislabeled as a collaborative culture. Leaders assume the lack of open conflict and a comfortable, congenial working environment signal a collaborative and effective workplace. Similarly, a working environment in which there are frequent and sincere attempts to keep everyone informed may be mistaken for a culture of collaboration. In such a culture, leaders use means like newsletters and email to communicate factual information, such as dates of events, changes in policies or procedures, the addition of new programs, and the status of new building projects. However, keeping people informed, even if done well, is not the same as deep, rich, and meaningful collaboration.

There may be those who believe that holding frequent interdepartmental or cross-divisional meetings or forming ad hoc committees in order to seek recommendations regarding specific issues is the same as collaborating. While leaders may go a step beyond merely keeping everyone informed by interacting in periodic meetings in which they answer questions and facilitate back-and-forth dialogue, this approach typically only minimally emphasizes joint decision making, shared problem solving, and mutual accountability—which are the hallmarks of true collaboration.

Quite frequently, a culture in which people seem to cooperate with each other willingly is viewed as a collaborative culture. People in various offices or even across divisional lines may readily share and support one another's initiatives, may share resources, or may even assist in completing tasks or serving students. However, simply supporting, sharing, or assisting each other still is not true effective collaboration.

If each of these views of collaboration falls short, what then is effective collaboration? What does a culture of collaboration look like? DuFour et al. (2008) offer the following definition of *collaboration*: "A systematic process in which people work together, interdependently, to analyze and *impact* professional practice in order to improve individual and collective results" (p. 464).

There are a number of key words in this definition that have important implications for developing a meaningful and effective collaborative culture. Notice the word *systematic*. Meaningful collaboration is a *systematic* process, not a series of random events, initiatives, and activities. In other words, meaningful collaboration is embedded in both the structure and culture of the everyday life of the institution. It is "just how we do things around here." In a true collaborative culture, people work interdependently; they rely on each other for success. Interdependence is a way of life in a collaborative culture— the cultural norm.

It was this view of collaboration that Jack Welch, former chairman of General Electric, was describing when he coined the term *boundarylessness* in the 1990 *GE Annual Report* (Hirschhorn & Gilmore, 1992). Welch used boundarylessness to describe a culture of openness within an organization in which people focus their talent, knowledge, and resources on solving problems and producing results, rather than walling off expertise within separate departments, each pursuing its own priorities and agendas.

As Leonard Berry and Kent Seltman (2008) point out, boundarylessness encourages staff "to step out of the organization chart box in which they work to connect with people in other parts of the organization whose expertise can add value in addressing the problem at hand" (p. 64). It is important to recognize that in an effective collaborative culture, people collaborate purposefully in order to *impact results*, not because they view collaboration itself as inherently good, or enjoyable.

The Power of Collaborative Teaming

How can leaders embed this type of meaningful collaboration in the day-to-day life of a university? The previous discussion of the concept of boundarylessness may point to the answer. Leaders of highly effective organizations accomplish potent levels of meaningful interdependence and synergy by utilizing the power of collaborative *teaming*. These leaders recognize that one of the most powerful tools available to them is the effective use of high-performing collaborative teams.

For decades, leading researchers, writers, and practitioners in all arenas of leadership and organizational development have recognized collaborative teaming as the basic organizational structure of effective organizations. In *Learning by Doing*, DuFour et al. (2010, p. 141) present a sample of such observations:

> Empowered teams are such a powerful force of integration and productivity that they form the basic building block of an intelligent organization. (Pinchot & Pinchot, 1993, p. 66)

> Influencers increase the capacity of others by asking them to work in teams with interdependent relationships. . . . We increase capacity when we work together rather than in isolation. (Patterson et al., p. 183)

> We are at a point in time where teams are recognized as a critical component of every enterprise—the predominant unit for decision-making and getting things done. . . . Working in teams is the norm in a learning organization. (Senge, Kleiner, Roberts, Ross, & Smith, 1994, pp. 354–355)

The challenge for college and university leaders is clear: to move institutions that have a long history of faculty working in isolation and capture the power of collaborative teaming. This will not be an easy task, but it is a necessary one, and one in which the benefits far outweigh the difficulties associated with undertaking such an essential cultural change. The fact is, it will simply be impossible to achieve the goal of enhancing student success if campus cultures continue to reflect a culture of individualism and faculty working independently in isolation.

The Mayo Clinic: An Exemplar of Collaborative Teaming

Most college and university leaders proclaim that student learning is central to the university mission—its core purpose. Yet there are vast differences between institutions that effectively *operationalize* student learning as a core purpose and those that do not.

The Mayo Clinic—one of the most highly regarded brands in health care—is unique in no small part because of its relentless emphasis on and superior effectiveness at putting patients at the center of its mission. In an industry typically built around a cadre of highly independent specialists loosely tied to a facility that supports their professional activities, Mayo is distinctive in its laser-like focus on collaboration in service of superior patient care. The Mayo Clinic is built on two primary core values:

> An aspirational value (the good of the patient) and an implementation value (medicine as cooperative science) . . . . The Clinic epitomizes the phrase "values-driven organization." Should it ever lose its core values, it is destined to become an ordinary institution. (Berry & Seltman, 2008, p. 51)

Glenn Forbes, CEO of the Mayo Clinic in Rochester, Minnesota, speaks of the clinic's commitment to putting the patient first when he writes,

> What makes Mayo Clinic distinct is that we have said, "The needs of the patient come first," from the beginning. Over generations, we have driven the needs of the patient into our thinking about how policies were developed. We've driven it into our thinking about how we structure ourselves and our governance and how we allocate resources. We've driven it into our thinking when we recruit people and form staffs. We've driven it so broadly and deeply into our management and operations that it becomes part of a culture. Thus, when we bring an issue forward, it's not a thin layer of, oh yes,

that was the marketing mantra that somebody thought
of last week. No, this is driven much more deeply into
the fabric of the organization. That's what makes us different. (Berry & Seltman, 2008, p. 20)

Can university leaders speak about putting student success at
the center of university culture with such conviction and passion?
Equally important, are they able to organize and execute the work
of the institution in a way that reinforces and supports that focus on
student success? Remarkably, the leaders at the Mayo Clinic remain
consistent in putting the needs of the patient at the center of everything they do by operationalizing this statement of principle. They
consistently address the key question of how to do so. And at the
Mayo Clinic, the answer to that question is, by capturing the power
of *collaborative teaming*.

Teamwork isn't optional at the Mayo Clinic. Berry and Seltman
(2008) point out that not everyone would fit in at Mayo. People
who would not fit in include those with the following characteristics:

Those who prefer to work independently, covet personal
acclaim, lack interpersonal competencies, or seek to
maximize their income. . . . Collaboration, cooperation,
and coordination are the three dynamics supporting the
practice of team medicine at Mayo Clinic. (p. 65)

Jonathan Leighton, a Mayo physician, makes the following
observation:

The Mayo culture attracts individuals who see the
practice of medicine best delivered when there is an
integration of medical specialties functioning as a team.
It is what we do best, and most of us love to do it. What
is most inspiring is when a case is successful because
of the teamwork of a group of physicians from different specialties; it has the same feeling as a home run in
baseball. (as cited in Berry & Seltman, 2008, p. 52)

The Mayo Clinic serves as an exemplar for college and university
leaders who (1) value student success and (2) believe that they can

best address issues related to improving student success with collaborative teamwork. Berry and Seltman (2008) succinctly summarize
the culture at Mayo:

> Individual staff members—from physician to custodian—
> become active team players to serve patients' needs
> because treating complex illnesses requires the diverse
> expertise available from all personnel and the support-
> ing infrastructure. To work at Mayo is to be on the team.
> (p. 65)

Developing a culture reflective of a professional learning community
in institutions of higher education can be done. If the Mayo Clinic
did it, so can colleges and universities. At the Mayo Clinic, the needs
of the *patients* come first. Isn't it possible to create a campus culture in
which the needs—particularly the academic needs—of *students* come
first? The Mayo Clinic is committed to meeting the needs of patients
through unsurpassed *collaboration*. Certainly, colleges and universities
can create a collaborative culture that focuses on the needs of students.
Like the Mayo Clinic, colleges and universities can create a culture
in which no one individual is big enough to work independently of
others, recognizing that the combined wisdom of one's peers is greater
than any individual's. At the Mayo Clinic, collaborative teams tackle
difficult problems through a process of collective inquiry—seeking
out and trying best practices—and they judge the effectiveness of
their attempts through a collaborative analysis of results rather than
whether or not they simply like it or enjoy it. The processes of collective inquiry into best practices and the collaborative focus on results
creates a culture of continuous improvement—the hallmark of any
learning organization—at the Mayo Clinic. It is both desirable and
doable for colleges and universities to create such a culture.

Prerequisites for Team Effectiveness

A number of prerequisites must be met if collaborative teaming is
to be truly effective. Among these is a clear, widespread, and deep

understanding of collaborative teaming—what it is, what it looks like in daily practice, and how it differs from merely working together and getting along. A common vocabulary, a deep understanding, and clear expectations regarding the use of collaborative teaming are essential if everyone is to contribute.

Another condition is a commitment to directing, supporting, and monitoring the work and effectiveness of each team—team by team, task by task. Fullan (2001) cautions, "Collaborative cultures, which by definition have close relationships, are indeed powerful, but unless they are focusing on the right things they may end up being powerfully wrong" (p. 67).

Simply organizing departments into collaborative teams will do little to ensure success. Success comes from the quality with which teams perform the *right* work. Teams must have a clear understanding of what they are to do—how they are to function day in, day out, and most important, how their work directly enhances student success. University leaders must constantly and consistently connect the *why* with the *what*. Absent clear and focused direction, collaborative teaming minimally impacts student success. And while specific team tasks differ between academic and nonacademic areas of the university, the goal of improving student success and the lens through which teams view their work must be the same for all divisions and all teams across the university community.

A Passionate and Persistent Focus on Enhancing Classroom Success

It is unreasonable to think that colleges and universities can significantly impact retention and graduation rates without focusing on what happens in classrooms. Obviously, the nonacademic aspects of the university are important and play a critical role in the quality of student life, but a student's classroom experience and the quality of interaction with his or her professors form the core of a student's college experience and determine, to a large degree, whether or not the student stays in school and does well. Vincent Tinto (2012) makes this point when criticizing most institutional actions to improve student success as being largely "an uncoordinated patchwork of actions," with most efforts "situated at the margins of students' educational life." He writes:

> They have neglected the classroom, the one place on campus, perhaps the only place, where the great majority of students meet the faculty and one another and engage in formal learning activities. Lest we forget, so-called traditional students, who enroll full-time in a residential college or university immediately after high school, make up only a quarter of all college students. Most students do not live on campus. A great many work while in college. . . . They go to campus, attend class, and quickly leave to attend to other obligations. For them, the experience of college is primarily the experience of the classroom. Their success in college is built upon their success in the classroom. (pp. 5–6)

How, then, can collaborative teaming enhance the academic performance of students? First, the division of academic affairs must organize into collaborative teams at all levels. While there is no one right way to do this, all institutions have a natural organizing structure. For example, the vice president for academic affairs / provost along with the college deans might form a collaborative team. Each dean and his or her department chairs can form a natural team in most cases. Departments should organize and function around the principles of effective teaming. In large departments, grouping professors who teach the same courses might be an effective way to team.

Regardless of how it's done, the key factor is the work of each team—what each team does and how they approach their work. What should academic teams primarily focus on? The answer is this: teams must work together and hold one another accountable for *discovering ways to enhance student learning*. Although each team will focus on a number of different issues and initiatives, effective leaders work to limit initiatives and focus the work of teams primarily on the things that will help more students learn more. DuFour et al. (2008) note that teams must collaboratively address three fundamental questions to significantly improve student learning.

1. What are the essential knowledge, concepts, and skills we want our students to learn and be able to demonstrate in each major and each course?

2. How will we know if students are learning?

3. How can we provide additional time and support to students who experience difficulty? And how can we extend the learning of students who demonstrate proficiency?

What Do We Want Students to Learn and Demonstrate?

Virtually every college and university has developed course outlines or catalog descriptions for each course. Curriculum committees vet and approve the courses, and most departments require individual faculty members to develop a course syllabus for their courses. Despite these measures, what professors *actually* teach students in each course varies greatly. Even within separate sections of the same course, the material taught often depends on the interests, expertise, or, in the worst-case scenario, the whims of the particular professor who is teaching.

In many classes, there is a disconnect between the planned curriculum and the taught curriculum—not to mention the *learned* curriculum! What students are held accountable for and what they actually learn depends to a great extent on which individual professor happens to teach their section of the course. The popularity of such websites as RateMyProfessors.com reflects student attempts to glimpse what the classroom content of an individual faculty member will actually be, as opposed to an unreliable published course description.

Educational researchers, writers, and practitioners have recognized the link between student learning and clarity of learning outcomes for decades. The idea that students are more likely to succeed in the classroom if they know what they should learn should come as no surprise. In addition to a strong research base, clarity of learning outcomes for students reflects a good dose of common sense.

If college and university leaders want to enhance student success, they should organize the work of teams within departments and majors—especially professors who teach the same course. These academic teams should engage in deep, rich discussions aimed at clarifying the specific knowledge, concepts, skills, and in some cases, dispositions that students should learn in every course.

This is a huge departure from the way many colleges and universities traditionally function. Putting student learning and student success first, as our first priority, requires that we begin to question some long-standing sacred cows within the academy—and this is no easy task. Here we face essential questions: Do we have the will to consider, as a teaching faculty within a specific major or discipline, the essential skills and knowledge we expect that each student who completes a specific course—regardless of section or individual professor—will master? Are we willing to hold ourselves accountable, as a teaching faculty, for ensuring that every student is equally well prepared for the next course in the sequence or for higher-level courses? Are we willing to consider the possibility that students' learning difficulties may not always reflect their lack of ability or inclination but instead indicate differences in the relative effectiveness of various professors' teaching methods?

This is not to say that course teachings should be perfectly uniform or that professors should teach in a lockstep manner. Certainly, academic freedom and professional expertise provide great latitude in how professors teach their courses. However, determining *what* students should learn—the big ideas or major concepts of each course—should result from collaborative dialogue among professors.

It is not enough that academic teams of professors clarify the essential concepts for students to learn in each course, however. Once a collaborative teaching team within a unit has reached agreement regarding the core ideas or major topics that they expect students to learn in a particular course, then the team must grapple with the most effective ways to make that knowledge available to students in multiple ways—and at multiple times. Research reveals that individual students learn at differing paces and through differing modalities. Therefore, it falls to these teams to ensure that the fundamental concepts and knowledge of a course are accessible in various ways.

Students should have access to departmental websites to learn the main ideas of each course. Professors should review the essential big ideas with students at the beginning of each course. Periodically, throughout the course, when one of the essential big ideas is being introduced, professors should alert students to the relative importance of a particular topic or concept—essentially reminding them to pay attention.

Engaging academic teams in clarifying the major ideas, topics, and concepts of each course allows professors to collaboratively drill deeper into additional discussions that can enhance student success. For example, once the teams are clear on what students should learn in every course, they can address the question of what successful student work would look like. It is not unusual for professors to generally agree on what students should know or be able to do but hold very different expectations for student work.

When professors within the same department or who teach the same course deeply and collaboratively discuss what successful student work looks like, it can also lead to discussions around the issue of *common scoring*. Often professors who teach the same course engage in grading practices that vary greatly. For example, one professor might count the entire problem wrong if a student gives the wrong answer, while a colleague who teaches the same course might give partial credit. Different professors might give more weight to one particular factor than another. For example, one professor might put a lot of weight on homework assignments. However, common scoring of student work isn't a new idea for colleges and universities. Many, if not most, English departments now utilize common scoring in composition classes—to the benefit of both students and faculty.

Team collaboration around the big concepts or essential ideas and skills of courses can help with the pacing of lessons throughout the semester. Although the goal is not to have every professor who teaches the same course at the same point in the lesson each day, there should be some broad common pacing. It makes little sense for one professor to spend a couple of days on a topic and another professor teaching the same course to spend two weeks! If the discussions among faculty teams are deep, meaningful, and focused on clarifying what students should know and be able to do, the teams will enhance student learning.

How Will We Know If Students Are Learning?

Once collaborative teams have clarified, communicated, and most important, acted on what students should learn in every major and every course, they can then move to the next two questions: Are our students learning? How will we know? Teams address these questions through the collaborative development and use of *formative* assessments in addition to the more traditional summative assessments.

Formative assessments are assessments *for* learning—assessments that provide information to both the students and the professor and that assist students in their learning. Douglas Reeves (2000) provides an appropriate analogy to differentiate between summative and formative assessments. He notes that a *summative* assessment is analogous to an autopsy, in that one's health cannot improve as the result of an autopsy. In contrast, *formative* assessments are much like going to the doctor for regular checkups, where one can receive information to improve health. It is virtually impossible for educational leaders to plan for specific, meaningful, and focused assistance for students unless mechanisms such as formative assessments reveal *timely* information about which students experience difficulty and the skills with which they struggle.

Increasingly, researchers, educational writers, and practitioners recognize the power of formative assessments. Consider the following.

- Paul Black and Dylan Wiliam (2004) write, "There is strong and rigorous evidence that improving formative assessments can raise standards of pupils' performance" (p. 20).

- Rick Stiggins (2004) notes, "Studies have demonstrated assessment for learning rivals one-on-one tutoring in its effectiveness" (p. 27).

- Robert J. Marzano (2006) touts formative assessments as "one of the most powerful weapons in a teacher's arsenal" (back cover).

- W. James Popham (2008) asserts, "Formative assessment is a potentially transformative instructional tool that, if clearly understood and adroitly employed, can benefit both educators and their students. . . . Formative assessment constitutes the key cornerstone of clearheaded instructional thinking" (p. 3).

In short, one of the most consistent research findings about effective teaching is the power of *frequent* monitoring of student learning.

Like virtually every aspect of effective instructional practices, the use of formative assessments is greatly enhanced when teams of professors collaboratively work together. Professors within the same department or major, and especially those who teach the same course, should collaboratively develop and analyze the results of formative assessments. Reeves (2004) refers to common, instructor-made formative assessments as the "best practice in assessment" (p. 71). When educators collaboratively analyze the results from commonly developed formative assessments, it enables them to create systems with multiple forms of assistance for students who struggle with specific concepts and skills.

Although there is common sense to the notion that frequent monitoring can guide both the student and the professor to better student learning, some professors may chafe at the power of a collaborative departmental team to insist on the use of effective formative assessments. Although it appears reasonable to question the practice of a professor giving only one end-of-course examination, which, by design, gives students little chance of improving their learning during the course, there will be faculty who insist that it is an overreach of the collaborative team to dictate course assessment practices.

It is vital that faculty engage with one another to deconstruct these arguments, and base decisions on data rather than on emotion or anecdote. While professionals in most fields enjoy a great deal of autonomy and latitude to determine their approach to work, most would consider it malpractice to refuse to use the most effective, proven practices. Again, the standard that academic deans and departmental leaders should use is this: if one's own son or daughter was enrolled in a course, what would one want for them? When viewed through this lens, certainly most would expect him or her to receive frequent feedback during each course.

Over time, it is likely that careful analysis of student success data from various sections of a single course will demonstrate that students who receive frequent and timely feedback are, in the long run, more successful. Effective collaborative teams systematically analyze data such as grade distribution reports and student success rates in subsequent courses to determine which teaching practices yield the greatest levels of student success. It is important that faculty teams rely on objective data and encourage openness to trying out best practices with evidence of successful student outcomes.

How Can We Provide Additional Time and Support and Extend Learning?

By their very nature, universities represent a culture of high expectations. Most courses are, and should be, challenging. At the same time, high expectations can be communicated in ways other than simply making courses difficult. Lawrence Lezotte (1991) observes that one way to assess the degree to which educational institutions hold high expectations for students is by examining how the organization responds when some students do not learn. A culture that simply accepts the fact that some students are not learning is one of low expectations.

It is not enough for faculty teams to collaboratively clarify and communicate what students must learn in each course and develop frequent assessments of their learning. Unless students receive additional help and support when they experience difficulty, all efforts to instigate real change in the classroom will prove insufficient.

What should additional time and support look like? What characteristics of student academic support reflect an approach that is both effective and appropriate at the college level? First, teams should collaboratively develop a systematic plan to provide additional assistance to students who struggle. The support plan should ensure that students receive *timely* support—that is, when they initially experience difficulty, rather than having to wait until late in the course. (This presupposes, of course, the implementation of an effective plan of formative assessments, which gives students and instructors prompt feedback that identifies the need for additional intervention.)

The support plan must be *flexible*, meaning that students move in and out of the support system as needed. Professors do not permanently place them in a program or reassign them to an alternative class. The plan should also be *directive*. Students should be required to seek support rather than simply encouraged or provided the opportunity. And last, the effectiveness of the plan should be continually *monitored*. There is a huge difference between implementing a plan to provide academic assistance to students and implementing an effective plan.

Institutions that effectively implement plans to assist students who experience academic difficulty employ multiple strategies, which may include such interventions as peer-tutoring programs or professionally staffed tutoring centers; the assignment of graduate assistants to courses that have higher-than-normal failure rates; the creation of learning labs in particular areas, such as writing, mathematics, and science; or the use of supplemental instruction and similar research-based strategies. While no university should guarantee that all students who enter will graduate, it is not unreasonable for college and university leaders to guarantee that it will provide all students with focused and effective academic assistance during their courses of study. It is unlikely that anyone will take educational leaders seriously when they proclaim that student success is the heart and soul of their institutional mission and then fail to provide a system of support for students who struggle with their studies.

Likewise, faculty should constantly strive to celebrate the success of students when they *do* learn. They should also work to extend and enrich the learning of all students, major by major, course by course, experience by experience.

In summary, collaborative teaming is the cornerstone of improving student success—and the first place to turn when capturing the power of collaborative teaming is academic affairs. After all, if everyone else provides excellent support for students, but students continue to fail in their academic pursuits, there is little reason to think universities will improve student retention and graduation rates. Faculty teams must do more than collaborate—they must focus on the critical questions of student academic success: What do we want students to learn in each course? How will we know if they are learning those things along the way? And how will we provide additional time and support to those students who experience difficulty in their learning?

How Teams in the Nonacademic Areas Approach Their Work

While collaborative teaming in the academic arena is a critical component of enhancing student success, it is also the primary vehicle for supporting student success in the nonacademic areas of university life. Although the classroom is the primary building block of the student learning experience on any campus, roadblocks and red tape related to registration, course scheduling, academic advisement, fee payment, financial aid, or other enrollment or student support services can increase the likelihood of student attrition. Collaborative teams in the nonacademic areas must approach their work in much the same way as faculty teams but focus it on a different set of questions.

1. What do the data reveal to us?

2. What goals, if achieved, would lead to significant improvement?

3. How can we seek information about best practices that may help us attain our goals?

4. What tasks need to be done? When? Who will be responsible for each task?

5. How will we monitor and celebrate success?

6. Are we committed to repeating the process, day in and day out?

What Do the Data Reveal to Us?

The lens for decision making in a professional learning community is data driven. Effective teams don't rely on personal opinions, don't take the best guess, and don't prioritize the easiest or least onerous tasks. Data always guides their work, revealing those areas in which they can make the most positive impact on student learning. The nonacademic areas of any college or university are varied and complex, comprising a host of different functions. Still, most of these nonacademic operations have a direct, or at least an indirect, impact on the quality of the university experience for most students. While the functions of each individual office differ, how teams approach the work is always roughly the same.

Using the common lens of data-driven decision making begins when teams collaboratively analyze multiple forms of existing data on customer or student satisfaction, relative effectiveness of processes compared to similar operations at other institutions, numbers of transactions processed, similarities of common complaints, and so on. The collaborative analysis normally reveals a number of strengths. Teams should recognize and celebrate these, and work to determine the practices that have led to success.

At the same time, the data can reveal that there are areas that need strengthening, though not all of these will be equally important. The team should collaboratively analyze the data and determine which areas require immediate attention—which are the biggest problems—with particular emphasis given to issues that impact student success and the quality of their university experience.

What Goals, If Achieved, Would Lead to Significant Improvement?

The primary benefit of data is to inform practice and guide decision making. Once teams have analyzed data and identified strengths and areas needing attention, the next step is goal setting. They should clarify the specific goals they believe will result in significant improvement. In short, achieving goals—both short term and long term—is how teams close the gap between their current reality and what they are trying to achieve.

For goals to achieve their desired aim—that is, help improve operations to better support student success—each one must meet certain criteria. First, the goal must be derived from and supported by reliable data. It must be strategic and focused on the right thing—in this case, on improving student success at the university. The tasks and activities associated with the goal must have specific time lines and must be assigned to specific team members for completion. The goal must have a measurable outcome that enables the team to assess their success.

It is important that this outcome is more than simply the sum total of the team's tasks and activities. In other words, teams accomplish tasks and activities to achieve results, and the results are the stated goals. For example, the goal of an academic advising office might be to reduce by 10 percent the number of continuing students not registered for spring term classes by the end of the fall term. Meeting this goal may require a number of activities and tasks, including running weekly reports of nonregistered students, making phone calls to nonregistered students, and so on. But the goal is not making the calls or running the reports. The goal is the reduction in the percentage of students not registered for courses in the spring term.

How Can We Seek Information About Best Practices That May Help Us Attain Our Goals?

When developing the strategies to attain their goals, teams often discuss a multitude of options and then average opinions. That is, achieving consensus between the points of view of various team members is substituted for seeking out research-based, data-driven best practices. High-performing teams in a PLC always begin to determine new strategies by gaining shared knowledge about highly effective practices already in place, whether these are internal or external to the organization. Effective teams make a conscious effort to seek the best information about a particular issue or problem and develop solutions that merit further consideration for their particular campus.

Albert Einstein (2015) famously said, "We cannot solve our problems with the same level of thinking that created them." It is imperative that collaborative teams look beyond the boundaries of their own institution to seek solutions. For instance, a team appointed to improve freshman orientation practices would do well to consult with the national organizations for professionals in orientation and advisement, as well as high-functioning programs on campuses with similar profiles to the home campus. Successful programs would, of course, require some level of adaptation, but expecting teams to seek best practices to guide their own initiatives is an important element of team culture.

What Tasks Need to Be Done? When? Who Will Be Responsible for Each Task?

Successful teams organize for success. As noted previously, planning requires clarity regarding which tasks teams need to accomplish if they are to realize their goals. Obviously, all of the tasks must be completed prior to the date set for goal attainment, so effective teams plan backward, determining which tasks they must complete by specific dates.

Teams should also assign their members clear responsibilities for accomplishing each task. This step involves not only who will be responsible but also deep, rich discussion about such things as who should be involved and in what ways. They ask, "Who should be informed?" It is easy to derail important goals by failing to notify a key stakeholder of the plan or assuming cooperation without sufficient communication and negotiation. Teams that work together to troubleshoot time lines, project plans, and communication methods greatly increase their productivity and ultimate success.

How Will We Monitor and Celebrate Success?

The power of formative assessment isn't just for the classroom. Successful teams must also plan to periodically monitor their work along the way. How many have been involved in the production of annual goals and objectives, only to see those set aside for the year, never to be revisited? Goals are not useful as an idle exercise. Setting and achieving goals is how collaborative teams close the gap between the current reality and what they are trying to achieve.

High-functioning teams do not rely solely on an annual reflection of goal attainment. They use regularly scheduled meetings to follow up and report on progress toward goals. They keep to-do lists and numerical targets easily visible. Reviews of the data are made as weekly, monthly, or semester statistics become available. Mutual accountability among team members is expected and valued, so as they monitor progress toward their goals, they constantly ask, "Can I help?"

By its very nature, continuous improvement is a never-ending journey. How then can team leaders keep their teams motivated? Few things stimulate others as effectively as recognition and celebration for a job well done. Effective teams celebrate short-term achievements. Rather than *hoping* success will be recognized and celebrated, effective leaders make concrete plans for recognition and celebration along the way. Similarly, they carefully evaluate setbacks as they occur so they can adjust activities as necessary. Team members are mutually invested in the outcomes.

Are We Committed to Repeating the Process, Day In and Day Out?

Continual improvement is a journey, not a destination—a process, not an event. The process is cyclical in that every team must get started and then continually get better. The fact is, university leaders can significantly impact student success if they connect the power of collaborative teaming with research-based, data-driven decision making and if they stick to their knitting—that is, enhancing student success. We would do well to remember that even an organization like the Mayo Clinic—widely celebrated and recognized for its success—is never content to rest on its laurels. As the saying goes, for the best organizations, "good enough never is good enough."

Team Effectiveness: Team by Team, Task by Task

University leaders at all levels must continually monitor team progress. The traditional cycle of setting annual goals and evaluating whether they've been met at year's end is woefully inadequate. Effective leaders constantly monitor the work of each team—both the products of their work (what they produce) and their processes (how they do their work).

We know that humans learn at different rates and in different ways. The same holds true for teams. Not every team, both within academic affairs and in nonacademic areas, is equally effective. Just as with individual students, when teams struggle, they need timely support and direction. Monitoring how well teams are doing is a critical component of every leader's job, with the ultimate goal of enhancing each team's effectiveness—team by team, task by task.

However, monitoring team effectiveness is never enough. Systematic and timely monitoring must go hand in hand with planned and continuous support. Teams need to be constantly reminded of why they are working toward specific goals. They need clear directions and time lines. They shouldn't be left to wonder what they are supposed to do. Teams need the resources necessary for success. Leaders must provide teams with meaningful training, rubrics, and examples. In short, leaders enhance team effectiveness when they couple the monitoring with a high-quality, effective, and systematic plan of support. As noted earlier, this is what Elmore (2004) refers to as "reciprocal accountability."

Summary

College and university leaders who genuinely seek to enhance student success must realize that the traditional approaches to collaboration are simply inadequate and ineffective. Like leaders of other organizations, university leaders must work together to make collaborative teaming the structural and cultural vehicle to accomplish the difficult and complex work of organizational change. Together, senior leadership must organize the entire university—in both the academic and nonacademic areas—into high-performing collaborative teams. They must clearly and consistently articulate the work of each team, while monitoring, supporting, and celebrating the work of teams along the way.

Universities will never make significant progress toward improving student success, retention, and graduation rates by individual effort. The tasks are simply too complex. There is a ceiling that limits the impact individuals can make.

The best hope lies in the power of teams—people working together, interdependently, to achieve common goals and holding each other mutually accountable. As Schmoker (2005) reminds us:

> Other professions understand that collective efforts to improve, sharpen, and refine one's professional practices have a profound and palpable impact on quality and improvement. In science, industry, medicine, and technology, professional effort and advancement are continuously nourished and accelerated by learning from and working with one's colleagues; collective work and effort are the engine for improvement and a power—the power of *collective* effort—can enhance higher education's efforts to significantly enhance student success. (p. 140)

CHAPTER 6

Enhancing Student Success in a Culture of Continuous Improvement

The goal of continuous improvement . . . is not to simply learn a new strategy, but instead to create conditions for perpetual learning—an environment in which innovation and experimentation are viewed not as tasks to be accomplished or projects to be completed but as ways of conducting day-to-day business, forever. Furthermore, participation in this process is not reserved for those designated as leaders; rather, it is a responsibility for every member of the organization.

—Richard DuFour, Rebecca DuFour, Robert Eaker,
and Thomas Many

Enhancing student success is an ongoing process that requires university leaders to create a culture of continuous improvement—a culture in which collaborative teams analyze data, seek new knowledge, and work to improve results every day. In times of rapid change, the need to develop such a culture is more important than ever, and organizations that resist change rather than adapt are doomed to eventually fail or become irrelevant.

Two recent examples come to mind. Compare the fate of Blockbuster, the video rental chain, with the success of Netflix, a company that constantly works to find new ways to deliver its products to customers. Think also of Blackberry, characterized by many industry leaders as having exhibited a stubborn refusal to change, even in the midst of breathtakingly rapid innovation throughout its industry. When leaders at Blackberry finally decided they must change, it proved to be too late.

Leaders of traditional public and private universities can learn from these and other examples of the change-or-die environment created by the transformation of an industry. No longer do universities with traditional cultures and ways of doing things monopolize the offering of postsecondary degrees. For-profit universities, MOOCs, and other online purveyors of credentials and degrees aren't going away anytime soon. This fact, coupled with wave after wave of criticism regarding poor student success rates, makes institutions of higher education particularly vulnerable. Creating a data-based culture of continuous improvement will provide the surest road to success in such a rapidly changing environment.

Needed: A Conceptual Framework

Clearly, few university leaders would oppose overtly or publicly the general concept of continuous improvement. The challenge, however, lies in moving an institution beyond the simple recognition of the need to improve. It needs clear and specific processes and procedures aimed at embedding a culture of continuous improvement in every level of the organization. Of course, a prerequisite for successfully developing such a culture is a clear understanding of what a culture of continuous improvement looks like and how it operates on a daily basis.

What would a culture of continuous improvement look like in the real world of university life? How would people in every division and every unit approach their work in a culture built on the idea of continually getting better results? At its most basic level, the process of continuous improvement must become a way of thinking about how all levels of the organization approach their work. This way of thinking must be accompanied with an attitude of specificity and fidelity to primary goals and objectives. Those in leadership positions must be especially attuned to this approach to set the direction and monitor the progress of the institution. Others throughout the university are not likely to embrace the concepts and practices reflective of a culture of continuous improvement if university leaders do not clearly understand the process and model the practices themselves constantly and consistently.

Conceptually, a culture of continuous improvement relies on a firm commitment to a cyclical and therefore never-ending process driven by data. The process requires teams to search for and implement best practices in the university's various improvement efforts. While this is not the only way to conceptualize the steps in a process of continuous improvement, figure 6.1 (page 98) depicts one way of thinking that contains each essential element in a continuous and cyclical journey toward getting better.

Improvement of Student Success: A Data-Driven Process

Any continuous improvement process begins with an understanding of the organization's current circumstances. Effective leaders start with an accurate view of the current reality; they paint a data portrait of the organization. Therefore, a process of continuous improvement must commence with the intense and collaborative collection and analysis of available and pertinent data.

It is worth noting that prerequisite to this process is to view the facts and data objectively. It is not unusual for people to dismiss data with which they do not agree or that show them or their unit in a negative light. To be effective, leaders must base continuous improvement planning on the assumption that team members view data and facts objectively and without bias. The therapist Carl

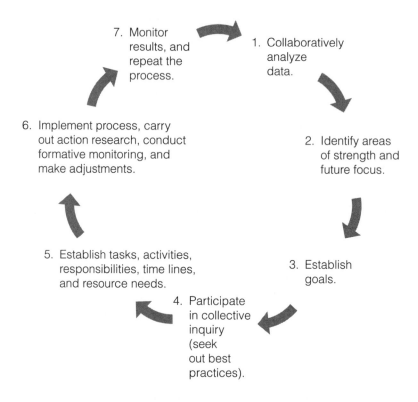

Figure 6.1: Continuous improvement process.

Rogers (1961) recalls how important it was for him in his own personal and professional development to shift his perceptions of facts. He writes,

> As I look back, it seems to me that I regarded the facts as potential enemies, as possible bearers of disaster. I have been slow in coming to realize that the facts are *always* friendly. Every bit of evidence one can acquire, in any area, leads one that much closer to what is true. (p. 25)

Similarly, Collins (2001) notes, "All good-to-great companies began the process of finding a path to greatness by confronting the brutal facts of their current reality" (p. 88).

A Systematic and Systemic Plan for Data Collection and Analysis

It's no secret that leaders at all levels in virtually every kind of organization develop plans to ensure that the things they value the most get done. It follows, then, that if higher education institutions truly mean it when they proclaim a universitywide commitment to improving student success rates, they will begin by taking a close look at current student success data of all forms and from a wide variety of sources.

The first step in a data-based decision-making process is to develop a specific plan to collect useful data. Rather than allowing data collection to be a random activity conducted by a few individuals (and actually used by even fewer!), it is important for colleges and universities to develop a detailed plan for the timely and routine collection and analysis of data.

Educators must collect learning data frequently. A yearly examination of summative data is not enough. Effective organizations collect relevant data along the way, viewing improvement as constant and ongoing, rather than as an annual event. Leaders must create a culture in which all levels of the organization routinely engage in reviewing formative data (data to use along the way) *and* summative data (data that reflect the end result).

Collaborative Analysis

In organizations large and small, it is not unusual for one person to not only collect the data but also summarize it and distribute the results to others. When conducted in this rather traditional manner, it is likely that data dissemination will have limited impact, at best. Obviously, data reports are necessary, but for the purpose of continuous improvement, decision making is greatly enhanced by *collaborative* data analysis by teams, conducted at multiple levels. A collaborative analysis of data captures the power of a collaborative team—mutually interested people who work interdependently in order to achieve improved results.

A collaborative team allows multiple points of view on data. Additional perspectives increase the likelihood that teams recognize instead of overlook significant data points. The actual process of collaboratively analyzing data can provide a learning experience that helps teams grow together, and the very act of continually reviewing data and working together can stimulate significant long-term organizational improvement. More important, creating a culture in which teams must collaboratively analyze data reinforces the basic organizational commitment to data-based decision making.

Multiple Sources of Data

Just as artists use multiple colors to create paintings, effective leaders rely on multiple sources of data to paint a data portrait of their organization. Rarely should leaders rely on one source of data for decision making. In any organization, the primary focus of data collection should directly relate to the organization's core purpose, and in the case of educational organizations, this core purpose is student learning and success, both inside and outside the classroom.

The learning data that teams examine need to be specific. Provosts, deans, department chairs, program heads, and others must dig deep into multiple forms of data, both quantitative and qualitative. For example, every term, academic leaders should review grade distributions by major, by course, and if applicable, by each section. In courses or sections in which they note unusually high failure rates semester after semester, the team needs to determine the specific knowledge, concepts, and skills with which students routinely struggle. This degree of specificity is fundamental to effectively focus improvement efforts and resources.

While they drill deep into the specific data, effective leaders must also step back and paint with a broad brush. They review enrollment data, retention rates, advising effectiveness, perceived quality of student services, student involvement, and graduation rates—program by program, major by major. And once again, they drill deep into those data, searching for specific trends and issues.

For instance, they examine data showing the number of students who change from one major to another. While it is perfectly normal for students to change majors, effective leaders mine the data to identify majors with an inordinate number of students dropping out of certain programs. Similarly, rather than looking only at aggregate withdrawal or dropout rates, effective leaders examine sections of courses that have higher-than-expected failure and withdrawal numbers, especially in comparison to other sections of the same course. Leaders undertake this rigorous analysis not to place blame but to shape interventions and deploy resources to those specific hot spots where they can improve student learning the most.

Comparisons and Patterns

Data, standing alone, are only facts. They must be viewed in comparison in order to become useful information. For example, if a university reports that its graduation rate is 52 percent, that is simply a fact. But what does it mean? Has the university improved its graduation rate? Is a graduation rate of 52 percent better or worse than others of similar size and student body composition?

Comparing longitudinal data is one of the most frequent and helpful forms of comparisons because it provides a picture of the effects of improvement efforts over time. Comparisons with similar institutions also help provide indicators of whether a particular university is exceeding, keeping up, or lagging behind the progress of peers. Many states are moving to creating formulas for their public institutions that use these direct comparisons as a basis for allocating state funding. Clearly, in those cases, there can be real and immediate impact to the bottom line, particularly if improvements or declines relative to sister institutions trigger the movement of funds from one campus to another.

Within a single campus, it can be particularly helpful for faculty teams, department chairs, and deans to compare data within a specific academic area, such as within a college, department, or major. For example, if the university offers fifteen sections of the same English course, it is important to review the grade distribution section by section. Do not expect the percentage of As, Bs, Cs, Ds, and Fs to be exactly the same in each section. What is the range of the rate of failure from the lowest percentage to the highest percentage in the same course with multiple sections? And what is the mean percentage, the median, and the mode? If a course has one section in which only 6 percent of the students received an F and another section in which 64 percent received an F, academic leaders should drill deeper into what is going on in the sections in which a large number of students are failing. Understanding the causes of failure is the first step in developing plans to improve student success in the course.

The larger point is this: academic and nonacademic leaders begin the process of improving student success rates by developing a systematic, cyclical, and timely plan to collect data from multiple sources and in multiple formats, in order to gain an accurate, specific, and meaningful understanding of their current reality.

Identification of Strengths and Areas for Future Focus

It's often said that the three most important words in real estate are *location*, *location*, and *location*. The corresponding words for a process of continuous improvement are *focus*, *focus*, and *focus*. Institutions of higher education, like most educational organizations, have limited resources. The question facing leaders of colleges and universities is, Where can an institution best use its limited resources in order to realize the greatest positive impact on student success?

It is not unheard of for institutions to implement student success initiatives that require significant resources of both time and money, yet are low-level strategies that fail to yield significant results.

Since university leaders need to focus their efforts on high-leverage strategies, the second step in a process of continuous improvement involves leveraging the collaborative analysis of data to identify specific areas of strength and areas of improvement that will have the greatest impact on student success. Such analyses must include both the academic and nonacademic areas of the university.

Identify Patterns of Strengths

If universities use the collaborative analysis of data for the purpose of improvement, it is only natural for teams and individuals to focus their attention on the weaknesses the data reveal—areas that need improvement. This is a mistake. The collaborative analysis of data should always begin with identifying areas of strength.

Generally, organizations comprise primarily people who work hard and engage in their work with a positive attitude. If the process of data analysis focuses only on weaknesses, over time, the process can have a debilitating effect, causing people to lose enthusiasm and energy. While simply identifying areas of strength is not enough to generate long-term organizational improvements, it is important that teams acknowledge what's going well by looking at existing areas of strength and effectiveness.

The team should engage in rich discussions focused on three fundamental questions. The first question is, What behaviors or structural changes contributed to success in areas in which the data indicate positive results? Discussions around this question allow team members to learn from each other and together. For example, consider a professor who has found ways to teach difficult concepts and skills and most of his or her students successfully complete the course. The data also reveal that other professors who teach the same course have exceptionally high failure rates. It is only natural to ask the professor with the high success rate how he or she got such positive results.

The second question the team should ask is, How can we reinforce the patterns of strength? It is important to make sure that success is more than an occasional event. By discussing areas of strength in deep and meaningful ways, teams can not only recognize what worked but also reinforce the behaviors and changes that contributed to the successes. Later, as the data indicate even greater improvement, teams should continue to address the issue of how to get even better!

The final question teams should ask is, Are there ways to expand our success? If a particular practice has produced successful results in one specific area, are there other areas in which team members can adopt or adapt that practice? A culture of continuous improvement reflects the commitment to expand best practices—even if the organization is already achieving positive results. The underlying concept of continuous improvement is to continually stretch the aspirations and performance levels of *everyone* in the organization—students, faculty, administrators, and staff alike. Expanding practices that work well to other areas within the university is one way to do this.

Identify High-Priority Areas for Future Focus

Effectively analyzing learning data should enable teams to target specific areas for improvement. Since it is virtually impossible to improve in all areas simultaneously, teams should review data patterns to determine which areas have the greatest and most urgent need— those areas that, if effectively addressed, will have the greatest impact on student success. For instance, are there general education courses that enroll large percentages of the student body but have low success rates? Increasing student performance in these courses would likely have a broad impact on overall retention and graduation rates.

Once high-priority areas of improvement have been targeted, it is important that both the plans and the data behind the plans are clearly and widely communicated throughout the university in multiple ways. By conveying a message that links the *why* (what the data show) to the *what* (the focus of improvement efforts), teams render the need to improve far more compelling. Linking improvement efforts to specific data patterns communicates a clear framework to target specific areas with limited resources. In other words, it provides a rationale for limiting initiatives by imparting the message, "We can't do everything we would like to do or even need to do, but a careful analysis of student success data has led us to believe that we can make the greatest impact if we focus our efforts on making significant improvement in these few areas."

Meaningful, Strategic Goal Setting

Goal setting is certainly not new to university educators. To a greater or lesser degree, it is at least an annual exercise on most American campuses. One of the great ironies of organizational improvement is that, on the one hand, nearly everyone agrees that setting and achieving meaningful goals is an essential element of organizational development, while on the other hand, there is also widespread sentiment that goal setting can be—and often is—a feckless endeavor and a waste of time.

There is a solid body of research that supports the role of effective goal setting in systemic improvement efforts. Denis O'Hora and Kristen Maglieri (2006) contend, "Goal setting is one of the simplest and most effective organizational interventions that can be used to increase employee performance" (p. 132). Goal setting is central to how effective leaders approach their work. According to Ken Blanchard (2007),

> Goal setting is the single most powerful motivational tool in a leader's toolkit. Why? Because goal setting operates in ways that provide purpose, challenge, and meaning. Goals are the guideposts along the road that make a compelling vision come alive. Goals energize people. (p. 150)

If developing a focused mission statement answers the *why* question and clarifies the core purpose of the enterprise, and if the collaborative development of a clear and compelling vision clarifies what the organization can become, then developing meaningful goals addresses the question of *how*—what steps are necessary and when are they necessary?—in both the short and long term (DuFour et al., 2010). To infuse goals with meaning, it is critically important that leaders link them directly to the organization's mission and vision at every opportunity.

Clear goals that are monitored on a frequent and timely basis support a results-oriented culture, helping create a culture of accountability. James Champy (1995) observes, "Vision is the rhetoric of inspiration . . . while goals are the rhetoric of accountability" (p. 54). It's difficult to overstate the importance of the accountability dimension that goal setting brings to the improvement process. Setting measurable goals throughout the organization provides not only a clear target for which to aim but also a way to monitor success along the way. Rather than simply hoping for results, use measurable goals to provide clear, specific, and data-based benchmarks.

With such a strong body of research validating the importance of the goal-setting process, why do people so often view the endeavor in such a negative light? As is true in most aspects of organizational life, when it comes to goal setting, leadership matters. The quality of leadership in the goal-setting process—especially monitoring and follow-through—determines not only the effectiveness of goal setting, but how stakeholders perceive the overall process.

Effective leaders understand that they cannot delegate the process of goal setting and forget about it. It must be much more than an annual activity that's sandwiched into the yearly performance appraisal process. In the absence of effective leadership, goal setting can quickly deteriorate into a purposeless exercise at best and a necessary evil at worst—a task to be completed and then quickly set aside, forgotten among the competing priorities of managing day-to-day operations. Leaders throughout the organization must demonstrate fidelity to established, approved goals. The lack of commitment to and follow-up on goals in the face of the constant barrage of daily to-do lists is likely behind the oft-repeated lament that the immediate tends to overshadow the important.

The good news is that the knowledge base about effective goal setting is deep. University leaders who are dedicated to enhancing student success utilize the power of this reservoir to further the continuous improvement cycle for the campus. While the particulars of effective goal setting vary, it should contain the following key elements.

- Is data driven and collaboratively developed
- Involves both short-term and long-term goals
- Identifies results rather than activities
- Limits the number of goals
- Is monitored, encouraged, supported, and celebrated

Data Driven and Collaboratively Developed

The development of an effective, systematic, and publicly reviewed process and calendar for goal setting is fundamental to the establishment of a data-driven culture of continuous improvement. Setting and achieving goals is where the rubber meets the road. Improvement doesn't simply happen on its own; change occurs in those areas where teams collaboratively develop and frequently monitor the progress of goals.

Leaders should broadly share the goal-setting process and calendar across the entire university community. They should refer to and emphasize it at every opportunity. Communicating and reinforcing the overall goal-setting plan not only enhances everyone's conceptual understanding of institutional priorities, but it also provides the extra motivation of peer pressure. Rather than keeping goals as private internal documents within individual units, this process ensures that all goals are public knowledge and may be publicly monitored. With the added expectation to report progress along the way, institutional goal setting and goal attainment can be a highly effective motivational tool.

The foundation of goal setting is the collaborative analysis of data, at every level, to determine which goals, if achieved, are likely to make the most significant impact. Simply accomplishing a goal has limited, if any, impact. The key is to accomplish goals that *matter*. If universities are to incrementally improve student success rates in a thorough and efficient way, every division and every department must pursue goals that, if met, will significantly impact student success and ultimately graduation rates. In short, goals must be meaningful and compelling.

Not only does a collaborative analysis of data from multiple sources help ensure that goals focus on the right things, but it also allows teams to establish baseline data. It is difficult to gauge progress with no clear starting point. The establishment of baseline data helps teams shape goals for measurable outcomes. It is virtually impossible to build a data-driven culture of continuous improvement without data-driven, collaboratively developed goals.

Meaningful collaboration plays another important role in the goal-setting process. Goal setting must be collaborative to ensure that goals across the institution interconnect and collectively reinforce each other. If goal setting is to lead to significant improvement, goals within each layer of the university must connect to both the layer above and the one below on the organizational chart. This ensures that goals are aligned throughout the university.

This interconnectedness can serve to reinforce the university's commitment to student success by communicating a clear set of institutional priorities. Requiring the development of interconnected goals that logically relate to overarching priorities helps ensure that the goals of all divisions and departments are meaningful and contribute to organizational improvement and enhanced student success.

Both Short-Term and Long-Term Goals

The process of goal setting should involve the development of both short-term and long-term goals. The creation of short-term goals provides smaller, more manageable targets by which progress can be judged. Moreover, the review of progress toward the smaller goals allows for adjustments to plans as more data are gathered regarding the relative success or effectiveness of various activities and approaches.

Short-term goals allow individuals to build confidence as they accomplish smaller steps along the way. Short-term goals make a long-term goal seem doable. When teams meet, recognize, and celebrate short-term goals, they create a winning attitude and boost confidence. Incrementally increasing confidence creates the expectation of success (Kanter, 2006).

Another important concept in the setting of both long- and short-term goals is granularity, which simply means that leaders break larger goals down in ways that become meaningful to the faculty or staff they have charged with achieving the goal. As an example, an effective leader helps members of his or her staff dig into the data so they understand that a 1 percent increase in the university's retention rate represents keeping forty-six additional students from the freshman to the sophomore year. Suddenly, what seemed vague becomes concrete, compelling, and doable. The goal becomes something individuals can participate in to effectively influence with a reasonable sense of ownership and responsibility. Individuals tend to dismiss goals that lack granularity as someone else's responsibility or as beyond their control.

Results Rather Than Activities

It is not uncommon for those who set goals to confuse them with activities. A true goal identifies a desired change in results and specifies the desired outcome. For that reason, the most effective goals tend to identify a quantifiable improvement in results—for instance, improving retention rates by a certain percentage or increasing the number of students participating in a particular academic support program.

But it can be tempting to substitute activities for goals, as teams so often assume that they can more easily control or predict activities than goals. Still, activities, such as creating a training seminar for graduate teaching assistants or developing new marketing materials for an academic support program, are a *means* of reaching a goal. Developing effective activities to support goal achievement is important, but accomplishing individual activities is not the same as attaining organizational goals. Understanding that goal setting is intended to impact results rather than to identify a series of activities is critical to developing data-driven, measurable goals.

Limited Number of Goals

Leaders should consciously limit the number of goals they work to achieve at any given time. DuFour et al. (2008) point out:

> One of the most consistent recommendations of organizational theorists and educational researchers alike is that leaders should limit the number of goals the people in their organizations are asked to pursue. . . . The adage "less is more" should prevail (pp. 161–162).

A limited number of publicly recognized goals reinforces the university's highest priorities. Having too many sends a message that institutional efforts are diluted, at best, or scattered and unfocused, at worst.

While leaders should not predetermine the number of goals, they should work with their colleagues to focus on a few high-priority targets that, if achieved, will advance the university's vision of enhanced student success. As noted previously, goals are generally effective only insofar as teams monitor them; fewer goals, carefully followed and tracked, contribute far more to institutional progress than many goals with no clear accountability.

Monitored, Encouraged, Supported, and Celebrated

It is not unusual for organizations to view goal setting as an annual event, often linked to performance appraisals or accreditation efforts. In either case, each year, every division and department head is expected to turn in his or her goals for the coming year and, at the end of the year, demonstrate the degree to which those goals were achieved. In the interim between setting goals and the year-end review, often little attention is paid to incremental progress toward the achievement of the goals.

One of the most visible ways that leaders communicate what they value—what they truly care about—is by what they monitor, or check on and pay attention to. The adage that "what gets monitored, gets done," already mentioned, certainly applies to goal setting. Effective leaders frequently monitor progress toward goal achievement, in effect communicating to their teams, "This is important, and I want to know how things are going." Ongoing assessment also provides leaders time to make adjustments and lend support or direction along the way when teams need it.

Monitoring goals involves much more than merely checking on how things are going. Just as analyzing data forms the basis for determining goals, it is also the cornerstone of goal monitoring. Even as teams focus on data, frequent analysis should involve deep, rich discussions about progress—or the lack of it. A regular review of progress toward goal attainment is an opportunity for leaders to listen, learn, and provide support and direction to encourage and contribute to success. Effective leaders use monitoring to send the twin messages of "This is a high priority for us," and "How can I help?"

Collective Inquiry: Research-Based Decision Making

Once goals have been clearly delineated, the question becomes, How do we best go about achieving our goals? The first step is to capture the power of collective inquiry by collaboratively seeking best practices.

Professional Learning Communities and Collective Inquiry

Earlier, the case was made that the best hope of improving student success in institutions of higher education is to implement the concepts and practices of a professional learning community. Each of these three words has implications for cultural change in virtually all organizations. For example, the word *community* implies working together rather than in isolation. However, simply working together does not ensure success. Teams begin the improvement process by seeking shared knowledge and learning together; hence the word *learning*.

Learning together has little impact without changes in behavior. The word *professional* has special implications for organizations that function as professional learning communities. These implications stem from what people expect from members of a profession. Much is expected of a professional person, but one of the most basic expectations is that his or her behavior—his or her practice—will be grounded in the latest and best knowledge available. Pfeffer and Sutton (2006) refer to this way of thinking as "evidence-based management." They write:

> Evidence-based management proceeds from the premise that using better, deeper logic and employing facts to the extent possible permits leaders to do their jobs better. Evidence-based management is based on the belief that facing hard facts about what works and what doesn't, understanding half-truths that constitute so much conventional wisdom about management, and rejecting the total nonsense that too often passes for sound advice will help organizations perform better. (p. 13)

This expectation is especially prevalent in the medical profession. Members of the medical profession must keep pace with a knowledge base that rapidly changes as new, proven knowledge becomes available. The same is true for lawyers and those in other professions. This expectation is so ingrained in the work of professionals that failure to utilize practices proven to be most effective can result in a lawsuit for *malpractice* (from the Latin term *mala praxis*—bad or unskillful practice).

Of all organizations, institutions of higher education should model collective inquiry—collaboratively seeking and applying the latest proven knowledge. However, the opposite seems to be true. Rather than actively seeking out research-based best practices in teaching, student services, campus operations, and the like, colleges and universities tend to turn within for answers; within a committee or task force, each person offers up his or her gut feeling or best guess for a possible solution. Obviously, there are many good ideas within every university setting, but looking only to one's own experience severely limits the chances of success.

Internal and External Sources of Best Practice

Rather than simply *encouraging* groups to seek best practices, university leaders must *direct* teams to seek best practices both internally (already occurring within the university) and externally (from other organizations—within and outside of higher education). For example, within universities, there are professors who get superior results in terms of student success rates. In courses with multiple sections, some professors may have high success rates while others have high rates of failure. It only makes sense to ask, "What can we learn from professors who are exceptionally successful?"

A word of caution is in order: some professors will simply dismiss the success of their fellows on the grounds that they are "too easy" or "give away grades." This is why collaboratively seeking best practice is so important. Working together, faculty can review research on effective teaching practices and on optimizing student learning.

When it comes to changing minds, few things are as powerful as a group honestly looking at data.

The university should not limit the internal search for best practices to classrooms. Some programs or initiatives, both within academic affairs and in other divisions, may be highly successful. An excellent example is evident in many athletic programs—especially at larger colleges and universities. When the NCAA began seriously monitoring athletes' graduation rates, colleges and universities responded by developing a host of initiatives to improve the learning and engagement of student athletes. Many of these approaches have been very successful, resulting in significant increases in the retention and graduation rates of student athletes.

Many universities have developed a number of effective support programs to assist students in their lives outside of the classroom. University leaders should continually examine exemplary programs across the organization to determine what they do that positively impacts student success rates. They should ask the question, "Is there anything we can learn that we can transfer to other areas within the university?"

Groups should also look externally for evidence of best practices. The interest in improving student success rates and the pressure to do so quickly is widespread across the United States. A quick Internet search reveals numerous practices that universities have undertaken to improve in areas including instruction, advising, student academic support, and student services. Moreover, research should not be limited to institutions of higher education. In particular, university leaders can learn much from the world of business and the medical profession. While it is true that colleges and universities are unique in their roles and cultures, this does not mean that no opportunities exist to learn from successful organizational practices outside of the university setting—especially in nonacademic areas of university life.

Transferability and Tweaking

Practices that have proven to be effective at one institution may not have the same positive effect at another. Every university has a unique history and culture. However, all universities have an inherent interest in enhancing student learning and, ultimately, student success. It only makes sense, then, that when seeking best practices, leaders choose to limit initiatives and implement those practices that offer the greatest potential for success at their particular institution—those most likely to achieve the best results.

Even promising practices or programs that seem like a good fit will likely need to be tweaked. Programs or practices rarely transfer uniformly from one organization to another, particularly if they go from outside higher education to inside. A fundamental tenet of the continuous improvement mindset is that practices need adjustments, not only with implementation, but periodically. Leaders and teams should constantly review formative data to determine where to make these adjustments. Every organization's mantra should be, "Get started—then get better!"

The Leadership Factor

The search for best practices through data analysis and collective inquiry is at the heart of every organization that strives to function as a PLC. Still, as important as this search is, these processes are no substitute for effective leadership. Programs are never a replacement for people. Universities are very unlikely to discover a program or practice that adequately compensates for weak and ineffective leadership. In fact, the opposite is true; effective leadership is a prerequisite for effective practices. The commitment to developing a data-driven culture of continuous improvement must begin with the senior leadership.

Organizing for Success

Leaders communicate what they value in a number of ways, but one of the most important is effective planning. Plans communicate to others what is valued by highlighting priorities and demanding specific actions. In other words, leaders do not leave important projects, goals, and improvements to chance. Inertia and a preference for the status quo are powerful forces. In the absence of specific, detailed implementation plans, it is highly unlikely that universities will implement changes and achieve important goals.

Planning for goal achievement can take many forms, but all effective planning formats contain the following common elements.

- Collaborative planning and development

- Constant connection to the *why*

- Major tasks

- Assignment of responsibilities

- Time lines

- Identification of resource needs and alignment of resource allocation

- Top-down and bottom-up planning

Collaborative Planning and Development

Again, a culture of collaboration is one of the defining characteristics of an organization that functions as a PLC. There is a direct correlation between the quality of collaboration that goes into the planning process and the quality of the plan itself—effective collaboration in, effective plans out! While it may seem tempting for someone to simply develop the plans singlehandedly (and it is certainly faster this way!), the quality of the finished product suffers. An individual working in isolation will not produce implementation plans of the same quality as those produced by an effective collaborative team. Moreover, even if the plan produced in isolation is superior, the group that had no say in its development will not be as committed to ensuring its success.

Constant Connection to the *Why*

Most people in most organizations are hardworking and very busy. How, then, can leaders combat the attitude that developing plans is just another piece of busywork—one more thing to do, turn in, and mark off the list? The most effective way to make planning relevant for leaders throughout the university is to constantly connect the planning process back to the goal that's driving it and the initial data that informed the decision.

One initial reference to why the university undertakes initiatives is never enough. Effective leaders constantly refer back to the institutional motivation and the underlying data with a recurring redundancy. The message is always the same: "Here is why we are doing this—here's why it's important, and here's what the data tell us. Therefore, we have collaboratively set these goals that, if accomplished, will have a positive impact on these data and help us become the kind of university we have said we seek to become."

Major Tasks

Major tasks will need to be accomplished if goals are to be attained. The senior leadership team should help collaborative teams identify and home in on the major tasks they need to successfully complete to accomplish each of the primary goals. Once they have agreed on the major tasks, the work teams can turn their attention to the question, What activities do we need in order to accomplish each task? It is unreasonable to think that divisions, departments, and other units will accomplish their goals unless they can agree on the major tasks they must accomplish and the activities necessary to effectively do so. Senior leadership plays an essential role in supporting collaborative team agreement on tasks and activities by first creating clarity on the major goals.

It is easy to get lost in the weeds of minutia. Effective teams identify major tasks, then move on to develop specific activities. Absent the clear definition of major tasks, it is easy for work to fragment around individual pet projects. In those cases, a flurry of busy activity may mask the reality that the major goals languish with no real progress toward measurable improvements.

Assignment of Responsibilities

Things only get done when there are clear lines of responsibility. Once leaders have delineated major tasks and the activities associated with each task, the question becomes, Who is responsible for making sure each task and the associated activities get done?

Clarity about these responsibilities also leads to clarity regarding plan monitoring. An important question that the senior leadership must address is, Who will be responsible for monitoring various tasks and activities? Clarity about who will be checking progress along the way is an important aspect of assigning responsibilities.

Transparency in assigning responsibilities increases peer pressure. When the entire group is aware of who is responsible for conducting each task and activity, the person who holds that responsibility is much more likely to finish those tasks, finish them well, and finish them on time.

As always, responsibility must align with authority. Despite the best of intentions, assigning responsibility for a task to a leader who lacks the supervisory or budgetary authority necessary to complete it will usually doom that activity to failure.

Time Lines

It is important that leaders have a conceptual framework—a clear understanding of how goals fit together to support larger priorities. Clear time lines can enhance conceptual understanding. It's easier to connect the dots when the senior leadership team makes it clear when everyone is to complete their assigned tasks and activities and how those tasks and activities intersect and connect.

Of course, there is a more practical reason for developing clear and effective time lines: there is often a logical order in which things must be done. Still, a word of caution is in order—if something can go wrong, it very often will. Don't screw things down so tightly that there is no wiggle room if something comes up unexpectedly, as it surely will. In this regard, it is critical that time lines be both flexible and realistic.

Identification of Resource Needs and Alignment of Resource Allocation

Even the most collaborative teams cannot accomplish important tasks and activities if leaders do not provide them with necessary resources (Elmore, 2004). Of course, colleges and universities do not have unlimited resources, and everyone, beginning with senior leadership must recognize the difference between resources that are nice to have and those absolutely essential to successfully complete particular tasks and activities. Because resources are limited, it is important that university leaders at every level be involved in developing the plan for goal attainment. It makes little sense to plan tasks and activities that university leaders cannot support because of budget constraints.

Top-Down and Bottom-Up Planning

Hoping for improved student success and *planning* to improve student success rates are two different things. When university leaders clearly articulate why enhancing student retention and graduation rates is important, every division, every department, and every unit can collaboratively analyze relevant data, set meaningful goals, and articulate tasks, activities, responsibilities, time lines, and resource requirements. Individual plans must become part of a larger whole.

For example, the university may set a goal to reduce failure rates within 1000-level general education courses by a certain percentage.

Next, the college of liberal arts might set a goal to reduce failure rates to no more than 15 percent in any of its 1000-level general education courses. Subsequently, when the history department analyzes its grade distribution data, it learns that the failure rate in its freshman general education history courses varies from 6 percent to 35 percent, depending on the course and section, and in aggregate is at 25 percent overall.

As a result, the history department team sets goals to reduce the failure rate, and based on a collaborative analysis of data, team members determine that they can make the greatest impact by focusing on their largest course, Early American History. Next, the department engages in a process of collective inquiry—learning what other departments both within the university and at other universities are doing to reduce failure rates. The department then develops a plan to identify tasks and activities, responsibilities, time lines, and resource requirements, as well as plan monitoring details.

The point is that the history department plan is *only one* improvement plan in the college of liberal arts. Every department makes similar plans, and these plans fit together to become the collective plan for the college of liberal arts. The college of liberal arts plan is only one of a number of plans within the division of academic affairs. Every academic college develops plans. The plan for academic affairs becomes part of the overarching university plan, which is made up of plans from every major division across the university. The plans fit together. In this sense, planning has become both top-down and, in response, bottom-up.

The Work: Implementation and Action Research

Of course, data analysis and planning are of little value unless they result in action. David Ulrich (1996) emphasizes, "The outcome of effective leadership is simple: it must turn aspirations into action" (p. 211). Effective organizations work diligently to close the gap between what they know they should do and what they actually do (Pfeffer & Sutton, 2000). This means that ultimately people have to roll up their sleeves and go to work! While effective planning is a prerequisite for success, planning without doing will accomplish little. Organizations that function as professional learning communities place heavy emphasis first on learning but then on doing (DuFour et al., 2010).

Enhancing student retention and graduation rates is difficult, complex, and incremental work. Because of this, it is crucial that university leaders provide ongoing support and at the same time monitor progress along the way. The fact is, leaders pay attention to what they value the most, and the primary way to pay attention—to communicate what is valued—is to provide support and monitor progress.

Loose on Approaches, Tight on Results: The Role of Action Research

Even when planning for improvement is done well, there are no guarantees. The best plan still only represents a group's best thinking at the time they made the plan. Once the implementation process is underway, groups may discover that adjustments are necessary. This fact alone makes the formative monitoring of progress absolutely essential. Those in leadership positions at every level must monitor the implementation of the improvement plans for which they are ultimately responsible and be willing to adjust along the way.

This is another example of the loose/tight principle. On the one hand, leaders must be somewhat loose about the strategies that their people employ in order to achieve significant results. On the other hand, they must remain tight on the end result they seek. In order to significantly and systemically enhance levels of student success, leaders must be loose on the means and tight on the end goal.

Additionally, monitoring progress in an organized and systematic manner is an effective way for leaders to develop a culture that values and supports *action research*. The basic question underlying action research is, What can we learn as we do the work? as opposed to,

What can we learn after we have completed the work? In a PLC with its emphasis on continuous improvement, action research helps teams learn from the entire process of getting better, rather than simply learning whether or not they have achieved results. An emphasis on action research reinforces efforts to create a *learning community* culture, one in which everyone—students and university faculty, staff, and administrators—is constantly learning and constantly seeking to improve.

Motivation and Inspiration

To be truly effective, leadership must touch the emotions (Goleman, Boyatzis, & McKee, 2002). University leaders who have undertaken the journey to significantly improve student success rates must do more than ensure effective data-based planning. They must also motivate and inspire. Moreover, motivation and inspiration should come not only from the top, as important as that is; leaders must be embed it at every level throughout the university.

The very concept of continuous improvement implies a journey that never ends. This fact creates a unique challenge for those charged with ensuring that the organization continually makes progress; how do leaders motivate and inspire others throughout the university to continually improve if the journey is never-ending?

Answering this question begins with an emphasis on creating small, incremental wins by supporting teams in their efforts to achieve short-term goals. Robert Schaffer and Harvey Thomson (1998) write, "There is no motivator more powerful than frequent successes. By replacing large-scale, amorphous improvement projects with short-term, incremental projects that quickly yield tangible results, managers and employees can enjoy the psychological fruits of success" (p. 203). Collins (2001) concurs, noting:

> When people see tangible results, however incremental
> at first, and see how results flow from the over-all con-
> cept, they will line up with enthusiasm. People want to

be a part of a winning team. They want to contribute to producing visible, tangible results. When they feel the magic of momentum, when they begin to see tangible results—that's when they get on board. (p. 175)

Leaders capture the power of creating small wins when they recognize and celebrate them. Kotter and Cohen (2002) point out, "The more visible the victories are the more they help the change process. What you don't know about is not a win" (p. 129). One of the most visible ways leaders communicate what they truly value is by what they publicly celebrate. It is impossible for any university leader to convince others in the organization that enhancing student success is a high-priority value in the absence of public recognition and celebration of progress in those areas. Kouzes and Posner (2006) emphasize the important roles public recognition and celebration play in motivating others: "There are few if any needs more basic than to be noticed, recognized, and appreciated for our efforts. . . . Extraordinary achievements never bloom in barren and unappreciative settings" (p. 44).

Cycle of Continuous Improvement

The ongoing cycle of continuous improvement is driven by an intense and passionate focus on results. As Ulrich (1996) points out, "It is not enough to declare an intent; leaders will have to deliver results" (p. 211). Organizations that are continually improving are usually led by leaders who are "fanatically driven, infected with an incurable desire to produce results" (Collins, 2001, p. 30). The critical question for leaders within universities that work to improve student success rates is this: Are more students learning more, and how do we know? The last step in a process of continuous improvement is an in-depth analysis of goal attainment throughout the university—in every division, department, and unit.

Monitoring results begins with a collaborative analysis of data. As the institution cycles toward the end of the process, however, the review becomes more summative in nature. In order to improve particular data sets, teams analyze the data compared to those they obtained at the start of the process and in relation to the goals they set.

Teams should conduct the initial summative review of results within each unit. Again, the data analysis should mirror the initial goal-setting steps; it should begin with identifying and collaboratively analyzing strengths that the data reveal. Only after working with areas of strengths is it time to focus the process on identifying and collaboratively analyzing the data that indicate areas of little or no improvement.

Teams should next come together and present their results to those who compose the larger unit. For example, the college of liberal arts may include a number of departments—English, history, philosophy, and so on. Leaders across the entire college should collaboratively examine results. Then, all of the colleges and units that collectively make up the division of academic affairs should repeat the process, and finally, the university's senior leadership team should collaboratively review the data from across all divisions and begin the process of goal setting for the next cycle.

A collaborative analysis of results is important for a number of reasons, but perhaps the most important is that it contributes to a culture of transparency. Organizations should seek and employ processes that promote constant transparency—processes in which there is a "clear and continuous display of results, and clear and continuous access to practice (what is being done to get results)" (Fullan, 2008, p. 14).

This is another example of simultaneous top-down, bottom-up leadership. The collaborative analysis of results flows bottom-up until the senior leadership ultimately gains a clear view of progress across the university and begins the top-down process of goal setting for another cycle.

Throughout this book, the case has been continually made that the concepts and practices of a professional learning community provide university leaders their best hope for significantly and systematically enhancing student success rates. DuFour et al. (2010) emphasize the connection between a focus on results and embedding a professional learning community culture when they observe:

> There is no recipe or step-by-step manual for becoming a professional learning community, but there are some things that must be done as part of the process. Using results to inform and improve practice is one of those things. . . . Inattention to results is antithetical to becoming a professional learning community. (p. 197)

Continuous improvement is a cyclical process. It is not a one-and-done endeavor. Those who are sincerely committed to creating a culture of continuous improvement realize that they will be embarking on a journey that never ends. When university leaders set out to improve student success rates, they must realize that the goal is not to get it right one time, but as Champy (1995) encourages, "get it right and make it better, and better, and better" (p. 27).

Every cycle will ideally identify strengths as well as areas that need improvement. Again, leaders throughout the university should publicly and sincerely celebrate the areas of strength and then recommit to improving. When this happens and people see the results—not only *their* results but the results of everyone—their confidence increases and they begin to believe. Confidence follows experience; it doesn't precede it. Even the smallest wins add up. Kanter (2006) reminds us:

> Failure and success are not episodes, they are trajectories. They are tendencies, directions, pathways. Each decision, each time at bat, each tennis serve, each business quarter, each school year seems like a new event, but the next performance is shaped by what happened last time out, unless something breaks the streak. The

> meaning of any particular event is shaped by what's come before. (p. 9)

Success is not a single event but rather an opportunity to stop, analyze, celebrate, recommit, and refocus everyone's efforts to keep getting better—continuing on a winning trajectory!

Summary

Planning to continually improve student success rates requires much more than a one-time initiative. It demands a way of thinking and, more important, a way of acting—year in and year out. Processes that prove effective generally contain the elements of data-based decision making, collaborative analysis of results, goal setting, and collective inquiry. The continuous improvement process insists on and supports seeking and using time-tested, proven best practices. Leaders should monitor the implementation and celebrate the success of activities designed to move the institution toward goal completion.

Engaging in continuous improvement is not reserved for the relatively few in official leadership roles; rather, it is for everyone throughout the college or university. Continuous improvement must be undertaken with fidelity; it must be the right thing to do rather than simply the required thing to do. To be truly effective, continuous improvement must be a way of life—simply "how we do things around here."

CHAPTER 7

Bridging the Rhetoric-Reality Gap: Helping More Students Succeed—As If We Really Mean It

Never mistake motion for action.

—Ernest Hemingway

Johann Wolfgang von Goethe said, "Knowing is not enough; we must apply. Willing is not enough; we must do." Goethe's admonition leaves unanswered the question, Do what? What would actually happen throughout a college or university *that really means it* when it proclaims that its highest priority is improving student retention and ultimately graduation rates? It is safe to assume that most, if not all, colleges and universities express a commitment to student success. One would not likely find an institution of higher education that promotes itself as an institution committed to making sure only a few succeed!

The issue of enhancing student success is not one of rhetoric but rather one of reality. Sadly, it is all too easy for the cumulative effect of countless acts of thoughtlessness to swamp the message of supporting student success. The leadership challenge is to close the gap between the rhetoric ("We are committed to helping our students succeed") and the reality that the data indicate ("However, more than likely, only about half of you will graduate").

Bridging the gap between the rhetoric of supporting student success and the reality of what students actually experience daily entails both structural and cultural alignments. If leaders do not effectively address these alignments, they cripple a college or university's commitment to enhancing student success, no matter how well intended. They must examine every aspect of the student and parent experience, from first contact with the university through graduation, in relation to the twin university goals of establishing high standards and supporting the learning of each student—course by course, skill by skill. Everyone within the university community must understand that making it difficult for students to fail is not synonymous with making it easy for them to succeed; enhancing student success need not equate to grade inflation or decreased classroom rigor.

Several researchers have authored reports, books, and articles about how to improve student success and, ultimately, retention and graduation rates. For example, in 2004, ACT released *Policy Report on the Role of Academic and Non-Academic Factors in Improving College Retention*. The report suggests that colleges and universities should:

1. Determine their students' characteristics and needs, set priorities among these areas of need, identify available resources, evaluate a variety of successful programs, and implement a formal, comprehensive retention program that best meets their institutional needs.

2. Take an integrated approach in their retention efforts that incorporates both academic and nonacademic factors into the design and development of programs to create a socially inclusive and supportive academic environment that addresses the social, emotional, and academic needs of the students.

3. Implement an early alert, assessment, and monitoring system based on high school GPA, ACT scores, other assessment scores, course-placement tests, first-semester college GPA, socioeconomic information, attendance records, and nonacademic information devised from formal college surveys and college student inventories to identify and build comprehensive profiles of students at risk of dropping out.

4. Determine the economic impact of their college retention programs and their time to degree completion rates through a cost-benefit analysis of student dropout, persistence, assessment procedures, and intervention strategies to enable informed decision-making with respect to types of interventions required—academic and nonacademic, including remediation and financial support. (pp. 21–24)

In his book *Completing College: Rethinking Institutional Action*, Vincent Tinto (2012), one of the United States' foremost advocates of improving college retention and graduation rates, identifies four conditions known to promote student retention:

- The setting of high expectations for students, so that they know what it will take to succeed

- The provision of adequate academic, social, and financial support

- The consistent use of formative and summative assessment and other forms of feedback to provide rich data to students, faculty, and staff about those conditions that help or hinder student success

- The creation of effective programs and activities to promote student involvement and engagement (p. 7)

Tinto makes several recommendations that seem to address this basic question: what would it look like if a university undertook retention activities as though they really meant it—as though student success really was the institution's highest priority. He suggests that addressing student success and retention must become a *primary* focus of the institution, not just "an add-on to the list of issues to be addressed" (p. 115). He reiterates that his framework for improved student success "places the classroom at the center of a student's educational life and in turn at the center of institutional action for student success" (p. 114). Further, he writes,

> Effective institutions employ evidence of student experiences and outcomes in their decision-making. They assess their actions and policies, modify them when necessary, carefully align them to the same end, and invest resources over the long term to achieve that end. (Tinto, 2012, p. 117)

Colleges and universities can look inside their own operations to see glimmers of improvement in student retention and graduation rates. As noted previously, one only has to look at the remarkable improvements in retention and graduation rates achieved with athletes to see evidence of effective academic support programs for students who are often at high risk of failure. Likewise, institutions have improved retention and graduation rates of special populations, such as students who experience English language difficulties. It's not as if leaders in higher education do not have a clue about how to enhance student success. However, garnering the widespread support necessary to scale up these efforts once again illustrates the challenges inherent in creating broad cultural change in an institution.

Aligning Institutional Structure and Culture to Enhance Student Success

Bridging the gap between institutional rhetoric and the reality of what students actually experience requires persistent, passionate, and effective leadership at every level. A key aspect of effective leadership is the ability—and willingness—to imagine and conceptualize what a true culture of student support throughout every aspect of the institution actually looks like. It's easier for people to get from point A to point B if they know where point B is and what it will look like when they arrive (Naisbitt & Aburdene, 1985).

While knowing what point B looks like is obviously important, imagining a culture of support involves more than simply having a broad conceptualization of what a culture of student success would look like. Leaders must unpack the institution's structure and culture into its various parts and develop a clear understanding of how each part impacts others and how, together, they impact the entire organization.

Aligning the Work

Unless leaders accompany their attempts to impact institutional culture with the requisite structural changes—changes in policies, procedures, rules, and relationships—systemic cultural change is virtually impossible. Those things that an institution truly values are ultimately revealed by what people do, rather than by what they say. Leaders who truly commit to improving student success rates are relentless in examining every practice, policy, procedure, and decision, and the impact of each on student success—both positive and negative.

It may be easier to accomplish than cultural change, but aligning an institution's structure, which is the result of decisions made over an extended period of time, is still not easy. Significant *cultural* change and purposeful *structural* change and alignment go hand in hand.

The term *disjointed incrementalism* (Lindblom, 1990)—sometimes referred to as the science of muddling through—describes how relatively large institutions are organized, particularly governmental and other publicly funded organizations like universities. In such organizations, structures and policies result from years of tinkering—small incremental changes over an extended period of time, often decades or longer. Because these structural, policy, and procedural tweaks accomplished specific purposes at different times, the structures became disjointed. That is, the pieces of the structure do not support and sometimes actually conflict with each other.

Aligning Roles, Responsibilities, Policies, and Procedures to Support Student Success

Because institutions of higher education reflect, to some degree, the characteristics of disjointed incrementalism, it is difficult to make substantive cultural changes without a deep, rich analysis of the institution's overall organizational structure, roles and responsibilities, policies and procedures, and everyday practices in light of how each might impact student success. As daunting as it may be, leaders must examine the roles, responsibilities, and policies of each office and each position in the entire institution to achieve meaningful structural alignment. Such an analysis should result in a sharpened realignment of responsibilities, policies, procedures, and most important, behaviors, with the overarching purpose of enhancing student success.

Obviously, each institution is unique. There is no single path to aligning institutional structure in order to enhance student success. There are, however, structural questions that every college or university should address. For example, who has primary responsibility for ensuring that practices at every level and in every office are aligned to support student success, both in academic and nonacademic functions? With whom does the ultimate accountability lie? Are policies and, more important, day-to-day procedures aligned to support and enhance student success? While it is true that everyone in every office has *some* responsibility to align their policies and practices (along with their attitudes and behaviors) to support student success, they must clearly recognize and understand who has ultimate responsibility to analyze the data reflecting the current reality and they must expect specific incremental improvement. Everyone should know where the accountability lies.

The primary responsibility for aligning a structure that supports enhanced student success resides with the senior leadership. Obviously, the president owns the ultimate responsibility, but he or she shares it with senior staff. For example, enhancing student academic success rests squarely with the provost / vice president of academic affairs. The vice president for student affairs is responsible for enhancing student support in most nonacademic areas. The vice president for finance and administration is responsible for enhancing student success within the financial arena, as well as areas such as student parking, safety, and other administrative services. Institutions have differing titles for the division responsible for external fundraising, scholarships, and alumni support. Regardless of the exact title, the vice president for this area oversees enhancing student success via support from external sources.

Depending on the size of the institution, there may be other divisions in which a vice president or other member of the senior leadership has responsibilities that impact student support. For example, many universities have a vice president for marketing and communication. The person in this role is responsible for frequently and consistently communicating the university's strong commitment to supporting the success of each student—from freshman enrollment to graduation.

While each of these leaders is responsible for organizing certain roles and responsibilities, reporting functions, and ultimately demonstrating results, it is critically important for all of them, led by the president, to work as a collaborative *team* committed to enhancing student success rates. They must work interdependently to improve student success by achieving common improvement goals for which they hold each other mutually accountable (Dufour et al., 2010). A senior leadership team is far more effective and impactful than individual vice presidents working in isolation.

Aligning Structure and Behavior

Of course, simply having the senior leadership collaborate will do little to improve student success rates unless their collaboration results in new behaviors and practices throughout the university—in each and every office across campus. A university's structure, policies, and procedures can be examined through the lens of the experience of students as they interact with one office after another. What is the quality of the experiences they encounter in each department or office? The bottom line is that at most institutions, student experiences are not uniform and consistent. In some areas, students primarily experience friendly and helpful people, along with procedures that are easy to understand and follow. In other areas, they more typically encounter unhelpful people who insist on leaping through a myriad of confusing and even contradictory procedural hoops. The issue that the senior leadership faces is why, despite the university's articulated priority to enhance student success, some office personnel behave rudely with students and develop rules and procedures that are frustrating, confusing, and often redundant. The answer is simply *because they are allowed to do so*!

Sharpening an institution's structural alignment and focus requires drilling deep into the work of each person in each office. Communicating expectations requires much more than simply expecting each office to support student success. Each member of the senior leadership must continually strive to close what Eaker and Keating (2012) refer to as the "expectation-acceptance gap"—the separation between what leaders expect and what they are willing to accept day in, day out.

One way for leaders to narrow this gap is through collaboratively developed protocols or expectations for each office. It is highly unlikely that individuals will align their behavior with an institution's expectations unless leaders consistently and frequently communicate, clarify, and most important, monitor those expectations. It is essential that all members of the institution see and believe that they are held accountable to a consistent standard, regardless of position or work assignment. Without it, faculty, staff, and administrators find it hard to achieve consistent levels of performance. The lack of accountability causes even those held to a high standard of service and support to experience frustration and sinking morale as they watch their peers in other areas fail to meet similar standards.

When it comes to routine administrative functions, it would be difficult, if not impossible, to overemphasize the importance of protocols and checklists—collaboratively developed, agreed-upon ways of doing things. These are an essential element of the structural (and cultural) alignment of institutions. These protocols ensure that team members deal with important parts of a process efficiently, reducing errors and omissions that create future stumbling blocks for students.

While some may resist the implementation of an established work-flow as implied criticism of their professional abilities or infringement on their professional autonomy, in fact, such checklists are central to guiding behavior in a wide range of organizations, including medicine, the airline industry, the military, the technology sector, and the construction industry, to name a few. Atul Gawande (2009), in *The Checklist Manifesto*, points out that organizational leaders do not always look for patterns of recurring mistakes and define potential solutions for correcting them. He writes:

> But we could, and that is the ultimate point. We are all plagued by failures—missed subtleties, overlooked knowledge, and outright errors. For the most part, we have imagined that little can be done beyond working harder and harder to catch the problems and clean up after them. We are not in the habit of thinking the way the army bomber pilots did as they looked upon their shiny new Model 299 bomber—a machine so complex no one was sure human beings could fly it. They too could have decided just to "try harder" or dismiss a crash as the failings of a "weak" pilot. Instead they

> chose to accept their fallibilities. They recognized the
> simplicity and power of using a checklist.
>
> And so can we. Indeed, against the complexity of the
> world, we must. There is no other choice. When we look
> closely, we recognize the same balls being dropped over
> and over, even by those of great ability and determina-
> tion. We know the patterns. We see the costs. It's time
> to try something else. Try a checklist. (pp. 185–186)

Whether leaders embed what is acceptable and unacceptable in checklists or simply establish these expectations as a baseline for behavior and attitudes, overt communication is essential to help people do the right things in the right ways. And people are unlikely to do so unless they know what those things are in the first place. How quickly do we expect to respond to student or parent inquiries, for example? What's a reasonable time frame for returning graded assignments? Under what circumstances is it OK to cancel a class meeting? It is up to senior leadership to clearly and specifically convey what supporting student success would look like—if they really meant it—and then to demonstrate their commitment to those standards in their own interactions with students and parents.

Aligning Behavior With Agreed-Upon Expectations

Of course, collaboratively developing checklists and protocols does not guarantee that everyone will follow them. In fact, it is likely that some personnel will not only ignore the protocols but also will behave in the exact opposite way. At this point, leaders must be willing to confront the behavior. How leaders react when someone violates the expected way of doing things sends a powerful message, not only to the person in question, but also to everyone else. Few things destroy a leader's credibility faster than an unwillingness to address an obvious problem (Burns, 1978).

Kerry Patterson et al. (2008) emphasize this point by noting,

The point isn't that people need to be threatened in order to perform. The point is that if you aren't willing to go to the mat when people violate a core value . . . that value loses its moral force in the organization. On the other hand, you do send a powerful message when you hold employees accountable. (p. 216)

There are a number of resources to help leaders learn to monitor and confront people who seem unwilling to change—to behave differently. Howard Gardner (2004) offers seven strategies leaders might use to change people's minds and behaviors.

1. **Reasoning and rational thinking:** Simply appealing to someone's sense of reasoning or common sense

2. **Research:** Providing factual evidence to support one's position

3. **Resonance:** Providing examples that are likely to resonate with a person's own experience

4. **Representational redescription:** Describing situations or data in different or in multiple ways

5. **Rewards and resources:** Providing rewards and resources to those who are willing to make the requisite changes

6. **Real-world events:** Providing examples of events that are occurring or have occurred in similar situations

7. **Requirements:** Ultimately, the leader may have to resort to their authority and require a person to behave differently

Kerry Patterson and his colleagues (2008) offer similar advice. They have synthesized the research of psychology, social psychology, and organizational theory and offer the following suggestions.

- Influence personal motivation.

- Enhance the personal ability of others.

- Harness the power of peer pressure.

- Find strength in numbers.

- Design rewards and demand accountability.

- Create structures to support the change and provide relevant information.

Regardless of the source, virtually all experts agree on one aspect of changing behavior: while *insisting* is rarely the first strategy they recommend, it is a tool that leaders must ultimately be prepared to use. As Daniel Goleman (1998) points out:

> Persuasion, consensus building, and all the other arts of influence don't always do the job. Sometimes it simply comes down to using the power of one's position to get people to act. A common failing of leaders from supervisors to top executives is the failure to be emphatically assertive when necessary. (p. 190)

Aligning Attitudes and Dispositions With Institutional Values and Commitments

Aligning behavior through clear expectations and written checklists isn't enough. The fact that people are doing the right things does not necessarily mean they are doing them with the right attitude—and with fidelity. Leaders must clearly articulate the attitudes and dispositions they expect of the administration, faculty, and staff of the institution.

At the most basic level, this means university personnel should say, "I *get* to teach or serve this student," rather than, "I've *got* to teach or serve this student." Individuals prominently display both the "get to" and the "got to" attitudes prior to each fall semester. Are they excited about the new academic year and enthusiastic because they *get to* start the new term, or do they seem rather depressed about the fact they *have to* start a new term?

The issue of aligning attitudes and dispositions with a mission to enhance student success causes leaders to ask the question, "I know I have some people under my supervision who have terrible attitudes toward students, but how do I go about changing a person's attitude?" Simply because expectations for attitudes are clearly articulated does not mean they will be exhibited by everyone, in every office, consistently with each interaction. One of the most frequent mistakes leaders make when they undertake attitudinal change is to focus on attitudes rather than behavior. There is virtually nothing a leader can say that will convince another person to adopt a new attitude. People's attitudes are the result of their experiences and the behavior they encounter. If leaders expect people to change their attitudes, they must create conditions that will provide them with new experiences. Kerry Patterson et al. (2008), in *Influencer: The Power to Change Anything*, contend that "the great persuader is personal experience . . . the mother of all cognitive map changes" (p. 57).

The question for leaders, then, is how to provide people with different experiences that will, over time, impact their attitudes. The answer is this: in order to gain new experiences, people must face the expectation to behave differently. To change attitudes, leaders must first focus on the behaviors that will result in those new experiences that will, in turn, influence people's attitudes (DuFour et al., 2010).

Aligning Training, Support, and Resources Allocation

Aligning institutional structures also means aligning training, support, and resources with efforts to improve student success rates. Not only are training and resources necessary for success, but they also send a powerful message throughout the entire organization, proclaiming, "This is what we value. This is what we care about. This is where we have chosen to invest our limited resources."

Exemplars are one of the most important resources, but they are often overlooked. They help others see what might be—that others are finding success and how they do it. This is the reason collective inquiry is one of the hallmarks of an organization that functions as a professional learning community. When collaborative teams search for the best practice currently in use—either within their own institution or in others—they can see more clearly what they should do. Examples of best practice can dramatically speed the alignment process. Simply put, people do not have to start from scratch if they first can see what others are doing successfully.

Aligning Personnel Selection, Placement, and Promotion

Aligning training and staff development for existing personnel in order to positively impact student success rates is important, but it is only half of the equation. It is equally important that senior leadership consistently and clearly emphasize the kind of personnel that the institution seeks to hire and promote. As Collins (2001) reminds readers, it's critical not only to get the right people on the bus but then to get the right people in the right seats on the bus. This is a particularly difficult task in the area of academic affairs, where people highly value and esteem academic credentials. University leaders should, of course, seek to hire faculty and administrators who have stellar academic records. However, at the same time, the leadership must constantly send the message, "We are seeking faculty who see it as their responsibility to help students succeed." During the hiring process, it is critical that leaders evaluate both academic credentials and the candidate's commitment to students to determine if candidates are likely to be on board with the overall mission of supporting student success.

While it is often difficult to know if a candidate's attitude is congruent with student support expectations, administrators and search committees should dig deep into his or her previous work background. They should personally contact references for insights into how well the candidate worked with students and colleagues.

Additionally, finding candidates who fit an institution's value system requires heavy emphasis on candidate interviews. It is helpful to develop a series of situational questions that require candidates to answer in more philosophical ways in addition to the more routine questions related to background and experience. Perhaps the interview schedule can include time spent with students; decision makers should carefully evaluate the students' feedback as a part of the hiring process.

In both background checks and interviews, university leaders must send a clear and consistent message to search committees that in addition to excellent credentials and experience, the university seeks to hire personnel who have the right attitude for working collaboratively with their colleagues to help students succeed in their university experience. It is better to hire people who initially possess these attitudes than to constantly work to convince people with great credentials but inappropriate attitudes and dispositions to change.

There are few aspects of academia with such an obvious disconnect as that between the rhetoric of valuing student success and the reality of academic promotion. In most institutions, it is possible that a faculty member is promoted time and again based on a strong publication record, even if he or she provides little or no encouragement or support to students—class after class, semester after semester. Promotion in the face of a general disregard for student success, when repeated time after time, sends a clear message, and there should be little wonder when people question what the university truly values. University leaders who value enhancing student success are relentless in their efforts to bring hiring and promotion policies and practices in line with this value.

Aligning Expectations and Actions With the *Why*

While clarifying what is expected of everyone can have a positive influence on how people behave, it does little to promote the *fidelity* of behavior—people behaving in certain ways because they truly believe it is the right thing to do. Faculty and staff will put forth extraordinary effort if they believe what they are asked to do is worthwhile. Effective leaders use every opportunity to tie behaviors, attitudes, activities, and initiatives directly to the institution's core commitment to improving graduation rates by helping each individual student succeed—both within and outside of the classroom.

Not only do effective leaders initially make a compelling case for what they ask people to do, they do so on a frequent, ongoing, and consistent basis. Articulating the *why* must be more than a periodic event or an advertising message that appears in a slick brochure. If leaders aren't careful, their efforts can appear to be mere public relations gimmicks. Bridging the gap between the rhetoric of why something is important and the reality of student experiences requires a constant and meaningful connection of purpose to action throughout the day-to-day workings of the institution.

Aligning Monitoring, Recognition, and Celebration

As was pointed out earlier, leaders communicate what they value by what they do, rather than merely what they say. Two of the most important ways leaders communicate an institution's values is by what they monitor and what they publicly celebrate. What gets monitored and what gets celebrated must align with an institution's core purpose, values, and commitments, or the rhetoric of enhancing student success loses all meaning.

It's not simply a matter of monitoring and celebrating the right things; it's also a matter of frequent and timely monitoring and public recognition. The "secretary of the month" award and the annual "outstanding faculty award" simply aren't enough. When leaders monitor and recognize people too infrequently, they create many losers and few winners.

Leaders must make meaningful efforts to monitor and celebrate an institution's core values, and they best communicate this meaning with how they use data. For example, if the data regularly reveal that a particular professor has an unusually high failure rate compared to his or her colleagues who teach the same course, and leaders do nothing with this information, then there is little value in monitoring grade distributions section by section, course by course, and major by major. The same is true for public recognition and celebrations. If time and again, a particular professor, team of professors, or a department exhibit extraordinary effort to help students succeed, resulting in a decrease in student failures and dropouts, then leaders must acknowledge and publicly recognize those efforts, or they will eventually lose all meaning. University leaders have only to look at recognition and celebration practices in college athletics to see the results when leaders truly value something.

Summary

It is highly unlikely that university leaders will systemically and significantly impact student success unless they lead the alignment of a clear and compelling purpose, key structural arrangements, behavior and attitudes, training, and resource allocation, along with monitoring and celebrating across the entire institution. It's critical that leaders have a clear conceptualization of what is involved at each of these steps and how each step is connected and impacts the others. Equally important, these interconnections must be clearly communicated at every opportunity. Those who set about leading significant structural change must recognize that just because they get it—they see the big picture—that does not mean that this holds true for everyone else throughout the organization.

CHAPTER 8

Improving Student Retention and Graduation Rates: The Undergraduate Experience

As every past generation has had to disenthrall itself from an inheritance of truisms and stereotypes, so in our own time we must move on from the reassuring repetition of stale phrases to a new, difficult, but essential confrontation with reality. For the great enemy of truth is very often not the lie—deliberate, contrived, and dishonest—but the myth—persistent, persuasive, and unrealistic . . . . Mythology distracts us everywhere.

—President John F. Kennedy

There are few colleges or universities that have not yet undertaken their own set of initiatives designed to assist students who experience difficulty in the course of pursuing their degrees. Most institutions at least pay lip service to the notion that they must do a better job of retaining and graduating students. Unfortunately, many of these support efforts have only limited success and may, in fact, be misguided or misdirected.

Institutions may, for instance, determine that their only road to improved student success rates is to focus on recruiting better students. Demographics (and economics) work against these colleges and universities as they pour more and more money into recruiting and retaining the cream of the crop—those students who would be likely to succeed regardless of how the institution prioritizes student learning. Only a very few schools successfully implement the enroll-better-students strategy.

Others have determined that they will make broad academic assistance widely available to students by implementing a variety of writing labs, math labs, or tutoring centers to help them succeed. Of course, such programs and initiatives are an essential component to any plan to enhance student success, but in and of themselves, they are inadequate. Absent a coordinated and integrated approach—a cultural change in the institution—the students who need them the most don't use these broad approaches or use them as a last-ditch effort, when failure is already inevitable and the additional help will not make a difference.

Finally, some institutions develop elaborate and expensive student support programs for special populations—perhaps for African American men, first-generation students, or adult learners. While these programs prove effective for these small groups of students, they are often too expensive to scale to the proportion necessary to really move the needle on overall university retention and graduation rates.

Why are these approaches—recruiting better students, creating broad support programs independent of the academic classroom, and implementing small boutique support programs—so popular? Perhaps because each of these reflect the notion that the solution to low retention and graduation rates is someone else's problem. Tinto (2012) refers to the propensity of institutions to take an add-on approach to improving student retention:

> While it is true that more programs are better than fewer,
> the number matters less than where the programs are
> situated in the educational life of the institution and how
> they are organized and aligned one to another. Merely
> investing in retention programs does not mean taking
> student retention seriously. (p 116)

Hiring additional staff to create even more programs will not significantly impact student success unless leaders carefully coordinate and direct them at the heart of the student experience. Tinto further notes:

> What would it mean for institutions to take student
> retention seriously? It would mean that institutions would
> stop tinkering at the margins of institutional life and
> make enhancing student retention the linchpin about
> which they organize their activities. They would move
> beyond the provision of add-on services and establish
> those educational conditions that promote the retention
> of all students, in particular in the classroom, the one
> place most actions have failed to touch. (p. 116)

What is needed is for institutions to approach the development of student success initiatives through the lens of the professional learning community model. Collaborative teams of faculty and staff must examine data and best practices to determine the approaches to student support that have the greatest probability of success for their campus. Together, they must create a culture in which every staff member not only understands the institutional commitment, but makes his or her own personal commitment to creating a college or university in which the learning and success of every student is the highest priority.

Beyond a Culture of Luck: Cultural Changes in Academic Life

If colleges and universities are to make a substantial, systemic, and positive impact on the academic success of students, they must face a difficult truth—for most students in a traditional academic culture, luck is one of the most important variables in their success, primarily the professor one is lucky enough to get or not get!

For example, in many cases, huge variations exist among grading practices—even among faculty who teach the same course. Some faculty members allow students to do makeup work, while others don't. Some accept late work; some won't. Some professors mark an entire problem wrong if the student has the wrong answer, even if the incorrect answer is due to a simple miscalculation; others give partial credit in such instances. Some give review tests prior to major exams, while others don't. All of these practices, and many more that have gone largely unexamined, significantly impact the success of students as they pursue their academic studies.

For the most part, when students are assigned a faculty member for a course, they are entirely at the mercy of luck. Registration times based on credit hours earned mean that students may have few options for faculty selection when it comes time to create their course schedule. Registration guides often list "staff" or "TBA" instead of the name of the specific faculty member teaching an individual section of a course. Faculty advisors may be assigned based on last name or on the whim of a departmental secretary rather than on an understanding of advising effectiveness. These seemingly minor day-to-day decisions about how the university operates magnify the impact of luck on the student experience. Skeptical? Talk to a faculty member or administrator whose own child is about to enroll for classes. Most of them will admit to intervening and guiding their own students toward the faculty they consider the very best. And few would be willing to allow their own son or daughter to simply accept the luck of the draw.

Leaders of colleges and universities must realize that although it is an extremely difficult and complex undertaking, they must examine every aspect of the academic culture of the institution. One of the great mysteries of higher education culture is the unwillingness to focus on academic areas essential to improving student retention and graduation rates. As the 2004 ACT report *Role of Academic and Non-Academic Factors in Improving College Retention* points out, "Postsecondary institutions cannot and should not ignore the principal contributions that academic factors make toward improvements in college retention and performance" (p. 10).

Tinto (2012) echoes the call:

> The classroom is the building block upon which student retention is built and the pivot around which institutional action for student retention must be organized. But while institutions have invested for years in retention programs, they have yet to significantly reshape the college classroom and student experience within the classroom. If we hope to make significant gains in retention and graduation, institutions must focus on the classroom experience and student success in the classroom and align classrooms one to another in ways that provide students a coherent pathway that propels them to program completion. (p. 125)

Such a focus is not for the faint of heart. It requires strong leadership and a willingness to analyze and act on academic data, as well as passion and persistence.

At a minimum, a close examination of the academic culture and practices of a college or university should focus on efforts such as ensuring consistent and clear student expectations in courses, frequently using collaboratively developed formative assessments, and providing students who struggle with systematic and timely additional time and support to ensure that the classroom experience is consistently of the highest quality and that every student has equal access to the support necessary for academic success. A more in-depth examination of these practices was made in chapter 5 in the discussion of the work of academic teams. However, the importance of faculty collaboration to create the strongest possible classroom experience for students is at the very heart of all efforts to improve undergraduate retention and graduation rates and therefore deserves revisiting.

Clarity and Congruence of Course Expectations: Essential Knowledge, Skills, and Dispositions

Simply put, a college or university is a *learning* organization, regardless of whether the people within it learn through research or public service programs. Any organization with learning at its very core must focus like a laser beam on the question, Learn what? Collaborative analysis and agreement about what is essential for each student to know or be able to do in each course should be at the heart of any university's effort to enhance student success rates. It is one of the first questions addressed by any organization seeking to function as a professional learning community.

Certainly, most colleges and universities publish course expectations in their college catalogues or in each individual professor's course syllabus—or both. However, anyone who has completed a four-year degree curriculum can attest to the gap that exists between the planned and printed curriculum and what is actually taught in each course. When asked what the primary determinate of course content is, many students answer that it depends on the professor who teaches the course.

In order, then, to have a positive impact on student success, efforts must be made to drill deeper and ensure expectations are clearly communicated to students at the beginning of each semester. Leaders must embed processes to ensure that faculty members align their instruction and assessment methodology with articulated course expectations that are published in course guidelines or course syllabi. While this point may seem obvious, one of the unique challenges facing institutions of higher education is the question of balancing respect for faculty autonomy with surety that students are actually taught the knowledge and skills that the university, through a collaborative process, has deemed *essential*.

A number of obvious benefits occur when universities engage in a process of using collaborative faculty teaming, as described in chapter 5, to clarify, articulate, and monitor the essential outcomes for each academic course. Such a process—if done collaboratively and with fidelity—has the following benefits (adapted from DuFour et al., 2010).

- Promoting clarity

- Communicating priorities

- Promoting viability by providing enough time for the high-priority learning to be effectively taught and learned

- Promoting ownership—ensuring that it is the collaborative faculty teams who identify the essential knowledge, skills, and dispositions for the course

The Use of Formative Assessment in Each Course

Collaborative faculty teams must lay the foundation for common expectations by clearly articulating the essential outcomes of each course and then aligning their teaching to the agreed-upon high-priority skills, knowledge, and dispositions. In the next step, teams must work to capture the power of formative assessments by making sure they assess students on a frequent and timely basis and provide them with specific and helpful feedback about their progress in mastering course content. As noted previously, there is a significant body of research—and a great deal of common sense—supporting the use of formative assessments. Popham (2008) notes:

> Formative assessment is a potentially transformative instructional tool that, if clearly understood and adroitly

employed, can benefit both educators and their students
. . . formative assessment constitutes the key cornerstone of clearheaded instructional thinking. Formative
assessment represents evidence-based instructional
decision-making. If you want to become more instruc-
tionally effective, and if you want your students to
achieve more, then formative assessments should be
for you. (pp. 3, 15)

While the research demonstrating the benefits of formative assessments within a specific classroom is compelling, there is also growing
evidence to support the idea that faculty teams can enhance the power
of formative assessments by collaboratively developing common
formative assessments for all sections within a course. There are a
number of reasons for this. When faculty team members who teach
the same course collaboratively develop formative assessments, they
are forced to refine their common understanding of the most essential
skills and knowledge taught in the course and reach a consensus on
what students should know and be able to do as a result of taking it.
When faculty teams collaboratively analyze the results of formative
assessments, they encounter data that show areas in which students do
well, along with areas in which they struggle. By identifying the latter,
faculty teams are able to make course or instructional adjustments
and plan for specific time and support in those areas. In short, by
collaboratively developing and analyzing common formative assessments, teams can use data to make a number of important decisions
to enhance student success—course by course, skill by skill.

Systematic Additional Time and Support for Students Who Experience Difficulty in Their Studies

Of course, providing clarity on essential knowledge and forma-
tively assessing student learning will do little to improve student
success rates unless those who experience difficulty receive additional

time and support. It is not enough to rely on individual faculty members to assist students. While many of them go to extraordinary lengths to help struggling students, there is only so much they can do as individuals.

Even more challenging is the fact that some faculty do not believe in providing students with additional time and support. The really tough issue in improving retention and graduation rates is not technical but philosophical. Some students learn from professors who conduct their classroom instruction from the point of view that it's their job to teach, but it's the student's job to learn, and students who choose not to learn must accept the consequences of their poor choices.

Of course institutional leaders, and especially the chief academic officer, must emphasize that such a teaching philosophy is antithetical to the values and commitments of the university that prioritizes student learning and success as the heart of its mission. Still, the fact remains that it is disingenuous for any educational institution that claims its core purpose is to help students be successful in their academic endeavors to then fail to create a system of interventions to provide additional time and support to students who experience difficulty (DuFour et al., 2010).

Research gathered since the mid-1970s consistently reports that effective learning organizations hold high expectations for student learning. And, equally important, one of the most effective ways to determine the degree to which an educational institution reflects a culture of high expectations is to examine how the organization responds when some students do not learn (Lezotte, 1991).

To provide systems of additional time and support that significantly impact student success in a positive way, college and university leaders have to promote the collaborative development of programs and initiatives that possess certain characteristics. Plans for providing students with additional time and support should include the following characteristics.

- **They are systematic.** To be truly effective, any plan must be universitywide, collaboratively developed, multilayered, and not dependent on the individual faculty member to whom students are assigned. In other words, effective plans declare, "At our college or university here is what happens when students experience difficulty in their learning, regardless of what course they are in or the professor to whom they are assigned."

- **They should be a result of collective inquiry into best practice.** Rather than simply making decisions based on personal experiences or anecdotes about what to do to provide students with additional time and support, the process should begin with teams collaboratively seeking out best practices from other institutions. While no two colleges or universities are alike, initiatives and programs that have been proven successful at other institutions can be tweaked to fit the culture of particular institutions. The first step in any collaborative process in a professional learning community is to begin by gaining shared knowledge of what works.

- **They should be timely.** A key to successfully assisting students is *early* interventions—not waiting too late to provide students with assistance. For some students, and depending on the academic record they bring to the university, this may be in the form of immediate support as soon as they enter college. For others, time and support must occur as soon as students begin to experience difficulty.

- **They should have specificity.** Systematic time and support must focus on specific skills and knowledge with which students are struggling, ideally tied to and embedded in a specific class, rather than broad, general support systems.

- **They should be flexible.** Because initiatives and programs that provide additional time and support for students focus on specific skills and knowledge, once students learn the content with which they are experiencing difficulty, they should be permitted to discontinue participation in the support program. Students should rarely be permanently assigned to a fixed program. Because time and support focuses on unlearned skills and knowledge, students move in and out of interventions.

- **They should be directive rather than invitational.** Students who experience difficulty with their learning must be directed to get help. This may be in the form of a course requirement, or it may be as simple as an individual professor telling a student what to do to get help. The point is, colleges and universities must do much more than *invite* students to get help, or *encourage* students to seek additional support. Faculty and advisors must intrusively *direct* students to the help they need to successfully master course content, and should create conditions to monitor and respond to the student's compliance or noncompliance.

- **They should be continually monitored for effectiveness.** Having a systematic plan to provide academic assistance to students who are having difficulty in their learning is not the same has having an *effective* plan. Once a plan has been developed, the critical question facing university academic leaders must be, Is our plan to assist students academically resulting in more students being successful?

Deep in the Curriculum and Instruction: Using Data to Improve Student Learning

One of the great ironies of university culture is that while university personnel value data in research and include the importance of data-based decision making as a topic in many of the courses they teach, they are reluctant themselves to use data to better understand what happens in various majors, courses, and individual classrooms. It is virtually impossible to improve student success in their academic pursuits unless university leaders—presidents, provosts, deans, department chairs, faculty senate leaders, faculty teams, and individual faculty members—are willing to use data to inform their decisions on the most beneficial and effective ways to improve student success.

As noted, one of the first steps university leaders can undertake to improve student success rates is collaboratively analyzing grade distribution data for individual courses. Obviously some courses are, by the very nature of the content, more difficult than others. By identifying courses with high failure rates, university faculty can either redesign these courses or embed systems of support as a regular part of the course. With the use of predictive analytics, advisors can steer students away from some courses or advise certain students to take the course later or with a lighter course load. Collaborative analysis of course data can also reveal the specific skills and knowledge students struggle with the most, thereby enabling educators to effectively target student assistance.

Further, once teams have determined the mean grade for courses with multiple sections, they can focus on specific classes with perpetually and unusually high failure rates. This allows deans and department chairs to make informed decisions about courses that they assign to particular faculty and professional development for those whose classes show a high failure rate over multiple semesters.

By predicting which courses will be abnormally difficult, faculty and academic advisors can help students make informed decisions about a particular load in a given semester—especially during the freshman year.

While academic initiatives directed at the classroom experience should be at the heart of efforts to improve retention and graduation rates, a focus on the academic experiences of students alone is insufficient. Veronica Lotkowski, Steven Robbins, and Richard Noeth (2004), the authors of the ACT *Report on Academic and Non-Academic Factors in Improving College Retention* write,

> Although many programs rely on traditional academic factors to identify students at risk of dropping out, our findings suggest that this approach may be limited and may miss students who are at risk due to other, non-academic factors. Furthermore, the findings suggest that retention programs that focus primarily on helping students master course content alone may only address immediate, rather than longer-term deficiencies. Students who master course content but fail to develop adequate academic self-confidence, academic goals, institutional commitment, achievement motivation, and social support and involvement may still be at risk of dropping out. (p. 10)

Certainly, nonacademic areas of the university also have a significant role to play in supporting the success of students. At a minimum, leaders should analyze the areas of student recruitment, orientation, pre-enrollment administrative and transition processes, orientation and bridge programs, student involvement opportunities, financial aid operations, the first-year experience, academic advising, and the use of predictive analytics to identify opportunities to improve the student experience and to reduce barriers to student success.

First Impressions: Recruiting

Recruitment messaging is perhaps the earliest opportunity to establish expectations that support the success of students who later enroll at the institution. In their earliest recruitment interactions, colleges and universities either deliberately or inadvertently send a variety of messages about what the institution values and how students can succeed. Together, these messages provide students with their earliest understanding of what they can expect from the university and what the university will expect of them.

Therefore, perhaps the first thing required of the senior leadership of a university is to develop a clear and concise message regarding student success that is consistent across every aspect of the recruiting process—message by message, advertisement by advertisement, phone call by phone call, recruiter by recruiter, visit by visit, interaction by interaction.

The questions senior leaders must initially face are these: How can the university best communicate to prospective students and their families that it is committed to high academic standards and also to supporting the success of all students? In a competitive environment where student and parents are bombarded with messaging, how can universities send a clear message that if students work hard and put forth the effort, the university will go to extraordinary lengths to help them succeed, both within and outside of the classroom? How can the institution consistently communicate this message throughout the university and in every aspect of the recruiting process? Leaders must develop a recruitment plan built around the message of high expectations for students coupled with an institutional commitment to supporting their success.

Developing a Clear, Consistent, Data-Based Recruitment Plan

It is important to remember that the *entire* senior leadership team ultimately contributes to the recruitment plan. It is tempting to fall into more traditional silo thinking—that the development of an effective recruiting plan is the responsibility of the vice president of the division that houses recruiting and admissions. However, every division within the institution touches prospective students one way or another—even if they do so in a limited or incidental way. The senior leadership team, working together, must examine every aspect of the recruiting plan and then hold each other mutually accountable for monitoring the implementation of the plan, every day, through every potential interaction with prospective students and their families.

A systemic plan for enhancing student success and, ultimately, graduation rates begins with an in-depth analysis and planning regarding the recruitment of students. Such thinking requires teams to inspect the entire recruiting process through multiple lenses, beginning with the views of students, family members, and the general public—through both lenses of how these groups view the university and their expectations, and the university's views and expectations of them. The goal is not merely to produce a recruiting plan but to develop a plan that consistently and clearly communicates the institution's commitment to high-quality programs and academic excellence coupled with a pledge to help students succeed in their academic and nonacademic pursuits.

Recruiting Students: The Limitations of an Ability-Based Mindset

Ask faculty how best to increase graduation rates, and a significant number will advocate simply raising entrance requirements, specifically higher ACT or SAT scores—even though data demonstrate little correlation between ACT scores and graduation rates, and the considerable negative effects higher entrance requirements have on overall enrollment. Despite the evidence, the message from some faculty members on most campuses is, "If you want more students to be successful in their classes and to ultimately graduate, then give us better raw material with which to work!" In some cases, those who fear the decline of academic rigor greet proposals for additional academic support for struggling students with hostility. Some faculty may perceive *increasing student success* as code for lower standards and grade inflation.

Such thinking represents what is known as an ability-based mind-set—that is, the sense that students' success depends almost solely on their innate ability, and since ability is unalterable and unequally distributed among the population, the university's job is to sort and select students who have the highest ability.

There are a number of flaws with this reasoning. First, the evidence for using ACT and SAT scores as predictors of future collegiate success is weak. Second, most colleges and universities already seek the best students they can attract, and the pool of students with high academic ability is limited. Every institution works hard to attract students with high ACT and SAT scores and grade point averages. The competition for these students is intense. No college or university would refuse admission to a student for being overqualified.

Third, while state legislatures increasingly move toward linking a share of funding to the academic success rates of students, a significant portion of state appropriations—and all tuition revenue— remains connected to total enrollment. To have a significant impact on retention, an increase in ACT/SAT by universities would need to be large—more than just a few tenths of a point. Attaining increases in ACT/SAT scores sufficiently high to increase graduation rates—absent any other university intervention—would likely have the net effect of lowering total enrollment and result in a decrease in state appropriations and tuition revenue. Such a strategy might possibly work for the largest or flagship public institutions, which usually are able to count on full enrollment regardless of the entrance requirements. However, a strategy of significantly raising admissions standards to improve student success is much more problematic for the smaller, publicly funded regional institutions.

While funding should not be the *primary* motivator to increase student success rates, it nevertheless remains a factor—an important one. Some faculty members take the position that they would prefer a smaller institution with more academically talented students, out of a (perhaps misguided) sense of confidence that they personally will not be the ones who will lose their jobs because of the decrease in funding that accompanies lower enrollments.

Too, some faculty sincerely believe that since ability is unequally distributed among the population, they cannot affect a student's chance of succeeding in college. This lack of self-efficacy is often reflected in an ability-based mindset rather than an effort-based mindset.

Recruiting Students Through a Different Lens: An Effort-Based Mindset

If a university culture—behaviors, attitudes, norms, and habits—is grounded in the belief that student ability is fixed and the primary prerequisite for academic success, then it makes sense to assume that the only way to improve student success rates is to recruit higher-ability students. This idea raises three interesting points. First, the inference to be drawn from such a belief is that what university faculty and staff actually do or provide will have little or no impact on student success. Second, taking such a position does not communicate a very inspiring message to prospective students, their parents, or the public at large. Finally, and perhaps most important, facts and research simply do not support the idea that universities can do little to help students succeed.

Even Frenchman Alfred Binet (1911), considered by most to be the father of the intelligence quotient (IQ) test, insisted that intelligence is not a fixed quality and that with appropriate practice and training, a person's intelligence can increase. Researchers, including Carol Dweck (2006) at Stanford University, have conducted extensive studies in the psychology of success—how one's mindset can profoundly increase the chances of success. Dweck's research and that of others has helped shift thinking from a fixed, ability-based mindset to a growth, or effort-based, one.

Comparing a fixed mindset with a growth mindset, Dweck (2006) writes,

> Malcolm Gladwell, the author and *New Yorker* writer, has suggested that as a society we value natural, effort-less accomplishment over achievement through effort. We endow our heroes with superhuman abilities that led them inevitably toward their greatness. It's as if Midori popped out of the womb fiddling, Michael Jordan drib-bling, and Picasso doodling. This captures the fixed mindset perfectly. And it's everywhere. . . . People with a growth mindset, however, believe something very dif-ferent. For them, even geniuses have to work hard for their achievements. And, what's so heroic, they would say, about a gift? They may appreciate endowment, but they admire effort, for no matter what your ability is, effort is what ignites that ability and turns it into accom-plishment. (p. 41)

Just as effort and success are inextricably linked, recruiting and retention efforts must build on an effort-based or growth mindset. The university that invests in student success wants to clearly com-municate the excellence of its programs, faculty, and resources, and the loftiness of its expectations and standards. This messaging must consistently couple the institution's high standards with its commit-ment to supporting the hard work and efforts of students. The goal is to ensure that the university speaks with one voice in saying that when students put forth the effort to learn and succeed, the univer-sity puts forth the reciprocal effort to help them succeed—whatever it takes. This is the kind of message students and family members want to hear. It is, frankly, the kind of message taxpayers believe they should be paying for. And, perhaps most important, it is the right thing to do if higher education is truly the road to improved quality of life and the future success of the nation.

Building Bonds: From Acceptance to Enrollment

Most college-level sports coaches recognize the importance of the period between the time a recruit commits to a particular program and when that student finally reports to campus. These coaches identify the importance of staying in touch and reassuring the recruit of their support and commitment. The goal is to make sure the recruit feels just how much the coaches are looking forward to having him or her on their team. This period—the period between choosing a particular university and actually arriving on campus—is equally important for the nonathlete. Leaders must give careful thought to the issues facing students, consider ways the university can support the transition from high school to the university setting, and establish the foundation for success in the first year and beyond.

The key to successfully addressing this critically important period is to view this time through the perspective of new students and their families. What are their needs? What are their concerns? What are they unsure of? Whom do they turn to if they have questions? To the degree possible, university leaders should develop ways to proactively address these concerns, and equally important, they must establish ways to connect students—and their families—with the university. While the recruiting period establishes initial connections with students and their parents, this period between acceptance and enrollment strengthens bonds and cements relationships. This is the period that crystallizes student perceptions and forms their attitudes.

Colleges and universities support students in a number of ways during this period. There is no one right or magical slate of activities to ensure student success. The secret lies in first recognizing the importance of this period, and second, in collaboratively developing, implementing, and monitoring a plan to help create the conditions for new student success.

"I'm Your One Go-To Person"

One of the first things university leaders should recognize is that students and their families have many questions—especially students of families with no previous higher education experience. The challenge lies in the fact that these questions tend to cover a wide range of issues, from housing to financial aid and from selecting classes to enrollment. If students and parents must track down the appropriate person in each individual office to gain answers, they may begin their higher education experience feeling frustrated and confused. The people they finally talk with can make matters even worse by being unhelpful and unsupportive.

The quality of these early interactions forms the basis for perceptions and attitudes that students carry into the freshman year and beyond. It is frightening to think that the response and attitude of a single person in a single office can so tremendously influence the overall perceptions of students and family members for the entire university. If early experiences with the institution send a signal that students perceive as unhelpful or uncaring, it becomes infinitely more difficult to later convince the student to reach out for tutoring or other forms of academic assistance.

Some institutions meet the challenge by reconceptualizing how to deliver basic enrollment services to reduce the perception of unnecessary red tape and bureaucracy. The concept of a one-stop shop for student services or of an assigned enrollment counselor can help students successfully navigate initial enrollment tasks by eliminating the need to contact multiple offices in multiple campus locations. If the university establishes a single point of contact for each new student, it can proactively provide as much basic information as possible. Perhaps more important, such an arrangement sends a powerful message to the student: "If you have any questions or concerns, contact me at this number or email address. I'm your one go-to person, and if I don't know the answer to your questions, I will find the answer and get back with you."

Some colleges and universities make this connection in print, others electronically, and some via telephone. Some institutions utilize multiple communication strategies. Regardless of the method of communication, they thoughtfully craft and articulate the messages to make them purposeful. Of course, it goes without saying that the key to success lies in the behavior and attitude of the university staff person acting as the student's go-to contact. Done well, however, this service demonstrates from the outset that the university is organized around the principle of student success, rather than administrative silos or organizational charts that make little sense to students and their families.

Communicating Enrollment Musts

There are a number of tasks that students must complete before the university allows them to register for classes, and virtually each of these items has its own specific due date. If students do not understand what they are required to do or if they think they have taken care of all requirements only to learn they missed an important due date, they can feel as though they are off to a rocky start. Institutions should strive to effectively communicate requirements that are *musts* and their due dates in multiple ways, and remind students as critical due dates approach.

The area of financial aid is particularly important. Financial aid carries with it a multitude of forms and deadlines, depending on the kind of assistance that students request. Much of the process confuses students and parents. Colleges and universities must make a special effort to clearly articulate the requirements for each type of financial assistance and respond to questions in a timely and helpful manner. The development of financial aid checklists can be especially helpful to summarize the essential tasks and the dates by which students must accomplish them. It is also beneficial to identify the tasks and dates that consistently seem to cause students and parents the most difficulty. Universities can use these data to pinpoint areas of communications and procedures in need of review and improvement.

In spite of the best efforts, students will miss important deadlines leading up to registration for classes. The issue for university leaders is initially to reduce mistakes, but once students make them, it becomes essential to limit the negative consequences by intervening to help

students and parents get back on track for enrollment. Leaders should
not seize on a missed deadline as evidence that the student is care-
less or not fit for enrollment at the institution. The time to teach
students about responsibility is not during enrollment and financial aid processes; in fact, these processes are inherently complicated
and difficult, especially for first-generation students. Certainly new
enrollees and their families deserve the same patience and assistance
that anyone else would expect when dealing with similarly complex
processes—such as filing federal tax returns!

Finally, leaders may find it helpful to complete a holistic analysis
of enrollment requirements and tasks—an enrollment map. It can
be an eye-opening experience for faculty or staff members to accompany their own sons or daughters through the actual enrollment
and orientation processes of their own institution! Absent enrolling
their own children, leaders may want to consider actually walking
through the enrollment process themselves, mapping the requirements, reviewing communications, and interacting with every office
themselves in an effort to learn what students and their parents
actually experience. They may learn that requirements conflict with
each other or due dates do not match to support different tasks. For
example, financial aid may arrive after the due date for registration
fees. In some cases, graduate schools may require students to provide
an undergraduate transcript, even if the student is a graduate of the
same institution where he or she is applying for graduate school.
Such processes and procedures send a terrible message to students
and their parents—that the university is unorganized at best, or
worse, doesn't care.

The Significant Role of Social Media

University leaders must recognize and take advantage of the significant role of social media in the lives of students. It's important
to provide students with information about connecting with their
fellow students. Many students will do this on their own, but others

may not be aware of the opportunity or may not know how to access the technology. Universities walk a fine line when using social media as a way to connect students to each other and to the university. Administrators must connect to the forum to provide appropriate oversight and intervention when necessary, but without co-opting the conversation in a way that silences students. Often, a mature young professional can provide accurate information to combat rumors and ensure discourse remains civil and within the bounds of university policy, all without distracting from the connections students are making.

Social media also establishes communication links with and among parents and other family members. Many colleges and universities find personal Facebook pages to be a useful tool for frequent and timely communications with parents. Parents find the university Facebook page a meaningful way to get answers and communicate concerns as well as positive experiences with university officials.

The key to using social media to interact with parents is to pay attention to what parents say and *then respond in a meaningful way*. For example, if a parent doesn't understand why a certain thing is happening, university leaders should carefully explain the reasons and, in many cases, check into a situation before providing a response. It is critically important not to ignore or trivialize parents' concerns or questions. Again, university administrators must walk the fine line to be responsive but not controlling or defensive. The goal, when possible, is to encourage significant parent-to-parent and parent-to-university interaction. Such interactions can be very helpful in terms of parents finding answers to frequently asked questions and discovering ways to support each other and their students during their college years.

Pre-Enrollment Support Classes

Even when students meet the enrollment standards for a college or university, they may lack skills that can help them succeed, particularly during the all-important freshman year. This is why many universities offer short, focused camps, institutes, or bridge programs designed to help students get off to an auspicious start.

Such sessions essentially preview academic life, standards, and requirements. They may include topics like note-taking skills, test-taking skills, how to access and use technology available to students, and how to use the library and other academic resources. The sessions also typically emphasize academic expectations, like the importance of attending every class and not falling behind in assignments. Perhaps the most important theme they communicate is the critical importance of student effort to their success, coupled with information about where students can turn for assistance when they experience difficulty.

Orientation Programs

Virtually all colleges and universities conduct orientation programs prior to the beginning of classes. What these programs entail varies widely. However, most orientation programs welcome newcomers, provide general information about the university, and develop familiarity with the campus layout through a series of walking tours. Orientation is normally the first time students meet with their advisor or advisors—at least formally. It is also when most students actually select and register for the classes in their first semester.

Because incoming students and their parents meet with a significant number of university personnel during the orientation program, it is important that all people involved understand their particular roles, the information they should provide, and the attitude they should exhibit.

The important themes of orientation should be consistent with the themes students and families encounter in the recruitment process. Every activity in the orientation process should underscore the theme of the university's high expectations for effort, personal behavior, and meeting academic standards in each class and major. It is critically important that student orientation assistants, university staff, and the faculty involved with the program all share the same message—that success is going to require hard work and effort on the part of every student. The goal should be to inoculate students against the inevitable bumps in the road that they will encounter and to reassure them that having to stretch to succeed is a normal part of the college experience—and they can do it!

A second theme that should run through the orientation activities is the university's commitment to providing multiple avenues for support when students experience difficulty in their learning. Orientation should be a vehicle for providing students with information about the multiple sources of help and advice, both academic and nonacademic. The institution should take care to simplify this information to the greatest extent possible; looking at university operations through the eyes of students and parents can reveal the places where confusion is apt to occur. The college experience is entirely new to students, and if it seems overly complex and difficult, that is because it is. Anything that university leaders can do to relieve anxiety and simplify the complex certainly helps promote student success—especially during the freshman year. They can particularly reduce unnecessary complexity in the process for assigning or changing academic advisors and to the procedure to access various kinds of tutoring programs on the campus.

The constant message must be, "If you will work hard and put forth the effort, we will provide you with additional help and support. Together, we can do this!" All leaders should consistently convey throughout the orientation program that they *care*, and that the proof is the wide array of programs and services designed to support students. During the orientation program, but also throughout the student's entire university career, university leaders should constantly assess the caring quotient—the total effect of the efforts to let students and parents know that the university cares about the personal welfare and academic success of each and every student.

Those who attend orientation sessions should leave with the belief that their future questions and concerns will be addressed in a prompt, respectful, and meaningful way. Rather than viewing students and parents as a nuisance, the overarching message should be, "We are partners on this journey. We care, and we are so pleased you are here!" During the orientation process, leaders must strengthen the trust that will be essential if they expect students to reach out for assistance once enrolled.

Directed Integration and Involvement

Students who become engaged in meaningful and significant ways with university life, especially if the engagement begins in the freshman year, are much more likely to do well and graduate. Virtually all colleges and universities provide numerous opportunities for student involvement; some campuses host literally hundreds of student organizations. Traditionally, university staff and advisors encourage student participation and involvement in clubs and activities, yet often find that a core group of students tend to have very high levels of involvement while a significant percentage rarely or never participate. The point is this: if integration and involvement during the freshman year is such a significant predictor of student retention and graduation, why leave them up to chance?

Of course, directed integration and involvement into university life requires a great degree of cross-departmental planning. Pre-college orientation activities must clearly state that this university expects student participation. Students must learn of all the options available to them and, ideally, understand that specific activities are essential to their experience—for instance, major events like the opening convocation or a special speaker. If the university articulates its expectation for a certain level of participation—if students are told, for instance, that they must attend certain activities or a certain number of activities—the immediate reaction of many will be to ask the question, "Or what?"

Therefore, the institution must develop a practical and easy way to monitor student participation. There must be systems in place to gather data about students' perceptions of involvement opportunities, as well as ways to receive student recommendations for improvement. Last, the university must develop some recognition structure to acknowledge and promote student involvement. Moving from a culture which gives freshmen the *opportunity* to become integrated into university life, to one which *directs* them to become involved is hard, complex work—especially on the front end—but the dividends can be significant.

Focused Financial Aid

Rising costs of education, greater access by first-generation and low-income students, and difficult economic times across the United States mean that virtually all institutions of higher education must find ways to support growing numbers of students facing significant challenges related to financial aid. The result is that the office of financial aid is one of the busiest departments on a college campus and plays a significant role in both the initial matriculation of students (often determining what new students believe their entire university experience will be like) and in their ongoing support beyond the first year.

Incoming students must find their way through a myriad of forms and applications required by both the federal government and by the institution. These forms, at best, are complex and often confusing. One requirement often leads to another; if the federal government selects a student for FAFSA verification, the paperwork and submissions increase in volume. Students of every family background, age, and circumstance—but particularly first-generation students—will have questions and will need easy access to someone who can help them. Therefore, the quality and effectiveness of interactions and the attitudes of those who work in financial aid are critical. Collaborative staff teams must step out of their departmental silos of financial aid processing, orientation, registration, and academic advising to view the process of applying for aid and scholarships through the eyes of the student.

Universities are often guilty of establishing processes and policies that have more to do with the structure of an organizational chart than the experience of a new student and his or her family. A collaborative team can use data and best practice to help the institution reimagine financial aid processes in ways that ensure students receive timely, consistent, supportive help that they can easily access through special enrollment counselors, dedicated call centers, and academic advisors with additional training in financial aid issues.

After the initial semester, a significant number of students leave the institution or fail to register for successive semesters because they underestimated the true cost of attending college and simply cannot make ends meet. Even students who receive grants, loans, or scholarships are often unable to stay once they learn the cost of textbooks, meals, or even gas for transportation. Students reaching the upper division may encounter internship or teaching assignments that further increase their attendance costs. Institutions find that many students drop out of their studies because they lack the relatively small amount of money to cover an emergency need, the cost of books, or added costs related to an internship.

This is another example of how every division within the university plays an important role in retaining and graduating more students. In this case, both senior leadership and divisional teams must think in creative and collaborative ways to create timely interventions for students who struggle financially. Many schools, such as Georgia State University, find that students could remain enrolled if they have access to a microgrant or scholarship of not more than a thousand dollars. Such small monetary investments can potentially reap impressive dividends in terms of enhanced student retention and ultimately graduation.

Getting Started: The Freshman Year Experience

Colleges and universities widely recognize the critical role the freshman year plays in student success, and most of them feature at least a few programs to support students through their initial year. Success in the freshman year builds students' confidence and serves as an important barometer of their likelihood of reaching graduation.

Because the first year is so important, university leaders should analyze each and every aspect of the freshman year experience and install multiple, proven practices and programs designed to help students successfully become sophomores. One thing is for sure—early intervention is critically important. The *ACT Policy Report on the Role of Academic and Non-Academic Factors in Improving College Retention* concludes, "Before any retention effort can begin, postsecondary institutions must devise ways to identify students who need help and assess the kinds of help they need" (Lotkowski et al., 2004, p. 11). While a focus on the freshman year experience should involve both academic and nonacademic initiatives, immediate, effective, and multifaceted academic support should form the core of any efforts to enhance the success of freshmen.

This is one of the times when creating a culture reflective of a professional learning community can reap huge dividends by keeping the institution committed to providing students with additional time and support when they experience difficulty. Most colleges and universities still have much work to do in this area. Fred Longenecker (2014), addressing findings from *The 2012 National Freshman Attitudes Report*, identifies areas in which college freshmen indicated they desired additional assistance. Seventy-five percent said they needed assistance to learn how to take college exams. Fifty-eight percent desired help to improve study habits, while 48 percent identified improving math skills as an area of need. Forty-four percent requested tutoring in one

or more courses, and 29 percent wanted assistance to improve reading skills.

These data highlight the opportunity colleges and universities have
to learn about areas of need through the eyes of their incoming
freshmen and to then tailor programs to assist them. Of course,
closely monitoring the effectiveness of these programs is a key element of any plan to enhance student success. Fortunately, a wealth
of resources reflects years of data analyses and best practices to help
institutions identify those programs most likely to increase the success of freshmen. The National Resource Center for the First-Year
Experience and Student in Transition was established in the early
1980s and since then has served as a repository of data, a source of
professional development and training opportunities, and a resource
for what works in enhancing the first-year college experience.

In *Challenging and Supporting the First Year Student: A Handbook
for Improving the First Year of College*, John Gardner, M. Lee Upcraft,
and Betsy Barefoot (2005) offer recommendations remarkably consistent with the values of the professional learning community.
Among them:

- Broad, institutional commitment from leadership,
  faculty, staff, and governing boards to align policies,
  courses, programs, services, and resources with the goal
  of supporting the first year of college

- An expectation that all efforts to improve first-year
  success begin with a focus on student learning, both
  inside and outside the classroom

- Recognition that cross-divisional partnerships are
  essential to promoting the success of first-year students

- An understanding that a delicate balance of both
  challenge and support is necessary to foster first-year
  student success; there must be a judicious mixture of

challenging students to achieve their educational goals while at the same time providing support for the task

- A commitment to communicate high standards and expectations for academic performance and personal conduct

Differentiated Advising

Researchers have identified academic advising as one of the key areas that universities should address in their efforts to improve student success—especially during the freshman experience (Lotkowski et al., 2004). This is no small challenge. Improving academic advising is a difficult and complex endeavor, particularly on large university campuses.

Because effective leaders realize that "clarity precedes competence" (Schmoker, 2004a, p. 85), they begin the process of improving academic advising by first clarifying exactly what the term means on their particular campus, in each office, and for each person.

At the most basic level, excellent advising begins with the simple recognition and belief that students need effective, beneficial help and advice, and every person is a potential advisor to every student in some way. Advising takes many forms, including guidance on courses, scheduling, and other aspects of the college experience, like financial aid and career planning. Many students need it, such as incoming freshmen, students who have declared a major, and others who are undecided on their major. Advising can even take the form of personal counseling.

Typically, the term *advising* refers to academic advising—mentoring students about their course of study, which classes they should take and when to take them, the academic discipline, and graduate studies or the world of work. Good advising requires a variety of skills, including knowledge of the discipline or major, an understanding

of the routine institutional forms and processes required for enrollment and registration, and the ability to effectively build relationships
with students.

Although virtually everyone recognizes the importance of accurate
and timely advising, the quality of advising is one area of university
life students routinely view in a negative light. Faculty and staff
hold a range of views on advising—and on the students they advise.
Many feel honored and privileged to affect the lives of students in
positive ways. Alternatively, some feel students should read the university catalogue and figure things out on their own, in effect saying,
"We need to teach them to grow up. We are doing them a disservice
by holding their hands and solving their problems for them." Not
surprisingly, students have several complaints—they cannot find out
who their advisor is, their advisor is rarely in his or her office, their
advisor does not seem to know exactly what students need to do,
and so on. Again, when it comes to the quality of academic advising,
institutional leaders must help the university move from a culture of
luck (students may be lucky enough to have a great advisor) to one
of certainty (students will get excellent advising if they attend this
college or university—we guarantee it!).

Differentiated approaches to advising can help. Students who have
not decided on a major—particularly freshmen and sophomores—
have different advising needs than students who know their major.
Effective academic advising programs recognize and address these
differences through the development of clearly articulated advising responsibilities assigned to the faculty or professional staff most
appropriate to work with those specific advisees.

While many factors affect the quality of advising, three key factors stand out: (1) clarity of expectations, (2) monitoring, and (3)
accountability. Clarity means leaders must not only be explicit about
the advisor role and job expectations but must also develop institutional transparency regarding degree requirements and university
rules, procedures, and expectations. Additionally, they must monitor

advising on a frequent and timely basis and in a meaningful way. However, monitoring, even if done well, has little impact unless leaders are willing to hold administrators, faculty, and staff accountable for high-quality advising and include it as a significant aspect of the university reward system. It is difficult to convince people that advising is important when leaders rarely monitor it, hold no one accountable for it, and don't include it in the university evaluation/ reward structure.

Why are efforts to improve advising so critical to student success? Aren't students notoriously close-mouthed when they need assistance and reluctant to ask for help? Actually, students usually *do* let on when they need help. More often than not, when students come to an administrative or academic office, they are saying, verbally or nonverbally, "I need help." Unfortunately, university staff members are often terribly shortsighted and assume that the student who has arrived at their office or their service counter simply needs to conduct a transaction. So, colleges and universities focus their attention on providing great customer service and taking care of transactions efficiently and quickly.

While it is true that often students simply want to conduct their business and move on, a more helpful way to view transactions with students is to assume every student who comes to any office for any sort of reason is at a crossroads. Actually differentiating between the two is a critical aspect of effective advising across an entire campus. Administrators, faculty, and staff should approach every interaction with students as though they are meeting the student at an intersection that has the potential to support the student in his or her educational journey, never missing an opportunity to intervene in a positive, meaningful way.

In other words, colleges and universities need to adopt a broad view of the term *advising*. If faculty and staff keep waiting for students to tell an academic advisor or faculty member they need help or support, their efforts at enhancing student success will fall short.

The fact is, students may see their academic advisor once a semester at best—just prior to registration. And many students simply cannot drop by a faculty member's office for a talk during available office hours. However, students visit various administrative offices every semester at numerous times. If colleges and universities view every one of those visits as an opportunity to support students beyond a simple transaction, and see the transaction in light of a student's larger goal of succeeding in college and ultimately graduating, a university could move from a culture of weeding out the weak and unprepared to one of caring, encouragement, and support.

Using Predictive Analytics

Increasingly, colleges and universities turn to predictive analytics (often referred to as *big data*) to guide decisions with the greatest impact on student retention and graduation. Many universities, including the University of Texas at Austin, Southern Illinois University, the University of Hawaii, Georgia State University, and Middle Tennessee State University, find predictive analytics an especially helpful tool for assisting students.

The business sector has led the use of predictive analytics for decision making. This is why, for example, major companies encourage shoppers to use their store or business loyalty card. The data that companies obtain from the use of these cards, along with other sources, are staggering. As Libby Nelson (2014) points out:

> This is how Amazon knows that people who buy *Harry Potter and the Sorcerer's Stone* are likely to buy *The Lion, the Witch, and the Wardrobe* and *The Hunger Games*. It's how Netflix recommends *House of Cards* to people who watch *The West Wing*. But, it's also used to predict more serious matters: whether Target shoppers are pregnant, for example. (p. 2)

This is how grocery stores, Home Depot, and hundreds of other businesses make decisions about what products to provide for shoppers. They use these data with astonishing specificity—to make decisions about product offerings, including brands, sizes, and colors, as well as how much of it to order. And these decisions vary from store to store depending on the demographics and purchasing preferences of a particular store's customers.

Colleges and universities find the use of big data helpful in a number of ways. By analyzing data from literally hundreds of thousands of students who attend a particular institution over many years, it is possible to inform decisions about those likely to drop out unless they receive academic and nonacademic support, the nature of the support an individual student needs, majors in which students are likely to flourish or flounder, appropriate course loads for particular students (especially in their freshman year), and courses that students should avoid or take later in their college experience.

Of course, such data can also be used in ways that are worrisome. With the emphasis in many states shifting from funding based primarily on enrollment to funding based primarily on retention and graduation rates, some colleges and universities may be tempted to use predictive analytics to sort out students whose data show they are in danger of not succeeding. Unless faculty and staff are careful in how they use these data, the analysis of them can create a self-fulfilling prophecy effect. That is, it's possible that some view these data and use it to reinforce their beliefs that some students are marginal and probably won't make it—resulting in the conclusion that they can do nothing to help the students, since the data show they shouldn't be at the institution.

Nelson (2014) points out that colleges and universities must strike a delicate balance when using predictive analytics. She observes:

> [College and university personnel] need students to believe that the trends they are projecting are real—real enough to get them to seek out tutoring help, or try a major where students with similar track records have succeeded. They also need the grant-makers and

administrators who hold the purse strings for support
programs to believe that pinpointing the students less
likely to succeed really will help them graduate. (p. 14)

Summary

University leaders who strive to shift institutional culture to a focus on student learning must take a broad, integrated view of retention initiatives and reinforce at every opportunity the notion that every division, office, and member of the administration, faculty, and staff has a crucial role to play. While a growing body of research outlines dozens of potential interventions, activities, and programs that may increase student success, there is no single silver bullet to improve student persistence and graduation rates.

Still, two facts stand out. Clearly, enhancing retention and graduation rates requires an intense, persistent, and deeply data-based focus on curricula and on the quality of classroom instruction, course by course. Once faculty teams identify the areas in which students consistently struggle, they need to develop a systemic, multilayered, and effective plan to provide students with additional time and support to help them succeed academically.

Second, institutions that are serious about increasing retention and graduation rates cannot be content with allowing each area to operate in its own silo, independent of one another and with no shared purpose, data, and accountability for success. While focusing on enhancing the academic experience of students is the necessary first step, leaders must support it with improvements in nonacademic support services. Without shared, coordinated, data-based efforts, the work to enhance student success rates will result in disappointment at best and failure at worst.

CHAPTER 9

Overcoming Barriers: Roadblocks, Detours, and Occasional Breakdowns

Conflict and disagreement are not only inevitable but fundamental to successful change.

—Michael Fullan

As mentioned in earlier chapters, changing the culture of any organization in significant, meaningful, and systemic ways is a difficult, complex, and incremental endeavor. It is often messy at best. Phil Schlechty (2005) refers to the challenge of re-culturing an organization as "disruptive change" because it "calls upon the system and those who work in it to do things they have never done" (p. 3). Others refer to cultural change as "second-order change"—innovation that represents a dramatic departure from the expected and familiar. DuFour et al. (2008) write:

> Second-order change is perceived as a break from the past, is inconsistent with existing paradigms, may seem in conflict with prevailing practices and norms, and requires the acquisition of new knowledge and new skills. . . . In short, real change is real hard. (pp. 92, 96)

Real Cultural Change

Real cultural change is real hard simply because people working within a familiar culture typically resist change and work to sustain the current environment. Most people are in favor of improvement as a worthwhile goal; it's change they are opposed to. To move institutions of higher education from a culture of sorting and selecting students to a culture of enhancing and supporting them requires leaders who accept the fact that successfully undertaking the challenge of cultural change will naturally create periods of frustration and, in some cases, even anger.

One of the prerequisites for successfully leading cultural change is not only the will to act, but the persistence to act even in the face of resistance and criticism. This doesn't mean leaders should not value feedback and be willing to make necessary changes in strategy. It *does* mean, however, that they must stay the course, relentlessly pursuing a worthwhile goal and not confusing constructive feedback with efforts to simply maintain the status quo.

Leaders should communicate not only that the goal of enhancing student success rates is a worthwhile one; they must also continually convey to their organization that it is, in fact, a moral imperative. Persistently and passionately focusing on cultural changes to enhance student retention and graduation rates *is the right thing to do*.

As difficult as leading cultural change is, leaders can make their efforts to re-culture institutions of higher education more effective by studying the change process and avoiding some of the common mistakes. For example, Kotter (1996) of the Harvard Business School identified eight of the most common mistakes that leaders make when undertaking organizational change.

1. **Allowing too much complacency:** Kotter argues that failing to establish a sufficient sense of urgency is fatal in any change effort.

2. **Failing to create a sufficiently powerful guiding coalition:** Leaders who work by themselves are rarely, if ever, successful in making significant and systemic cultural changes. Successful change requires a critical mass of people who work together to champion the change process.

3. **Underestimating the power of vision:** A powerful vision of what the organization can become inspires others to act. People within the organization must see a future that is compelling, doable, and inherently worthwhile.

4. **Under-communicating the vision by a power of 10:** Change efforts are doomed to fail without clear, consistent, and credible communication. DuFour et al. (2008) summarize three common communication errors.

   In the first, leaders underestimate the importance of communicating the vision. They mistakenly believe sending a few memos, making a few speeches, or holding a few meetings will inform people in the organization to change and recruit them to it. A second mistake is divided leadership. While the head of the organization articulates the importance of change, other leaders in the organization may tend to ignore it. The third mistake is incongruence between what key leaders say and how they behave. Strategies to communicate vision are always ineffective if highly visible people in the organization still behave in ways that are contrary to the vision. (pp. 99–100)

5. **Permitting structural and cultural obstacles to block the change process:** Leaders must recognize that a number of formidable obstacles typically block successful cultural change. These often include structures that make it difficult to act, insufficient training and support, supervisors or others in critical

positions who do not support the necessary changes, and information and rewards systems that do not align with what is needed to successfully fulfill the new vision. Leaders must address and minimize, or remove, these obstacles.

6. **Failing to create short-term wins:** People have an inherent need to believe that results are attainable. They do not wish to wait for success to occur in the long run. Leaders risk losing the initiative if team members have no short-term goals to reach and celebrate.

7. **Declaring victory too soon:** As Dufour et al. (2008) observe,

> There is a difference between celebrating a win and declaring victory. Until change initiatives become anchored in the culture, they are fragile and subject to regression. Handled properly, the celebration of short-term wins can give the change initiative the credibility it needs to tackle bigger, more substantive problems. Handled improperly, this celebration can contribute to the complacency that is lethal to the change process. (p. 100)

8. **Neglecting to anchor the changes firmly in the culture:** Structural changes, while necessary, by themselves are not powerful enough to drive systemic change. As Kotter (1996) notes, "Until new behaviors are rooted in social norms and shared values, they are always subject to degradation as soon as the pressures with a change effort are removed" (p. 14).

Other researchers and writers identify additional barriers to successfully changing organizations. For example, Ken Blanchard (2007) notes:

- Those leading the change think that announcing the change is the same as implementing it.

- People's concerns with the change are neither surfaced nor considered.

- Those being asked to change are not involved in planning the change.

- There is no urgent or compelling reason to change. The case for change is not communicated.

- A compelling vision about the future benefits of the change has not been developed or communicated.

- The leadership team does not include early adopters, resisters, and informal leaders.

- The change is not piloted, so the organization does not learn what is needed to support the change.

- Organizational systems are not aligned with the change.

- Leaders lose focus or fail to prioritize, causing "death by a 1,000 initiatives."

- People are not enabled or encouraged to build new skills.

- Those leading the change are not credible—they under-communicate, send mixed messages, and do not model the behaviors the change requires.

- Progress is not measured, and no one recognizes the changes that people have worked hard to make.

- People are not held accountable for implementing the change.

- People leading the change fail to respect the power of the culture to kill the change.

- Possibilities and options are not explored before a specific change is chosen. (pp. 203–204)

While changing the fundamental culture of any organization is difficult, doing so in colleges and universities is a particularly daunting task and has its own unique challenges. Some question whether it is even possible to change the fundamental culture of colleges and universities, particularly large, public institutions, at all—much less to lead the broad cultural changes required to significantly increase student retention and graduation rates.

Significant Barriers

There are a number of significant barriers within both the structure and underlying culture of most colleges and universities that make it particularly difficult to implement the concepts and practices necessary to enhance student success. One such barrier is the lack of agreement across the institution regarding its central purpose—the core mission. Higher education institutions have many differing— and often competing—interests, goals, and objectives. Tenure processes reward teaching, research, and service, but the university gives the greatest weight to research and publication. Leaders value administrative functions if they are efficient, yet rarely examine them to reveal their ultimate impact on student learning. Consumer-driven campus planning can overemphasize amenities that have little to do with student learning but may be popular recruiting tools. Universities often lack, with all the divergent and frequently disconnected activity that occurs on a college campus, a single, overarching purpose that gives focus, sets direction, and establishes clear priorities that enhance student academic success.

In their book *The New Corporate Culture*, Terrence Deal and Allan Kennedy (1999) write, "A key challenge for modern managers is finding a way to unite fragmented subcultures into a coherent whole around a common purpose" (p. 215). Deal and Kennedy argue that improved performance depends on an organization's ability to establish a clear and compelling purpose that has meaning for all participants in the system. Although these authors single out very large, very traditional corporations, such as IBM and Eastman Kodak, as particularly vulnerable to the mission disintegration that comes with cultural fragmentation, most institutions of higher education are equally at risk, as internal subcultures pursue their own preferred activities and priorities.

A second barrier to cultural change is the almost universal tendency for universities to attribute students' lack of success to conditions beyond the university itself. If students today struggle such that only approximately half graduate, the proposed answer to the problem (if it is even viewed as a problem) is usually to raise admission requirements—to get better students! Stuck within the paradigm of sorting and selecting only those students with the highest potential, many colleges and universities fail to significantly address the potential of support services and other strategies to enhance the chances for academic success for all students.

However, as noted previously, the U.S. Department of Education, as well as many state legislatures, prescribes college completion goals that define success in terms of a particular percentage of the population successfully completing a degree or credential. They set these benchmark goals without regard for any single institution's preference for a particular set of admission standards for its students—and without regard for the percentage of the population that might appear to meet those standards.

Despite the protests of many faculty, the expectation for a growing number of state universities is for higher education institutions to serve more than 50 percent of the population. Neither taxpayers nor politicians appreciate college improvement strategies that pit all public institutions against one another in an arms race to recruit and admit only the top 10 percent of the state's citizens. Instead, if learning is indeed the fundamental purpose of institutions of higher education, then the expectation is that all institutions—particularly public institutions—focus on creating a *learning* environment (rather than merely a teaching environment) that fosters academic achievement across the entire spectrum of the student population.

A third barrier to cultural change is professional isolation and the paramount value placed on individual autonomy that is characteristic of most college campuses. Faculties and their departments traditionally operate independently of one another. As Derek Bok (1986) observes:

> By common consent, no tenured professor should be forced to do anything. Very rarely is a department compelled to assume teaching responsibilities against its will. . . . This method of proceeding has a marked effect on the final result. Professors and departments are not obliged to cooperate with other units or individuals even when it might be educationally desirable for them to do so. (p. 39)

This culture of isolation makes improving student academic success an almost impossible task. In their book *The Knowing-Doing Gap: How Smart Companies Turn Knowledge Into Action*, Pfeffer and Sutton (2000) devote an entire chapter to outlining the ways in which destructive internal competition between individuals or departments within an organization tend to inhibit learning and creativity and lead to the failure to put knowledge into action.

Within the university setting, this often means that, when faced with choosing between what is good for student learning versus what supports the individual autonomy and happiness of faculty, leaders abandon practices that would enhance student success. Further, re-culturing colleges and universities to focus on enhancing the academic success of each student requires new ways of thinking that can challenge faculty who have entered the academy with a narrow interest in their own particular area of research or study. While academic interests and personal passions are important, they should not trump the core mission of the institution, which must be to help more students learn more.

Finally, a fourth and related barrier to cultural change is the tendency of universities to develop a series of independent silos or fiefdoms, so consumed with protecting their budgets that they have difficulty operating as a single institution committed to fulfilling a common mission. A growing number of institutions, as well as research associations, attempt to address this mentality, which conserves separatism and discourages open collaboration toward the shared objective of improving student success.

The collection, analysis, and dissemination of data are crucial to fostering enhanced collaboration. Faculty, staff, and administrators at all levels of the institution must examine routine practices to identify those areas that do and do not tangibly promote student success, and commit to reengineering those that block our best efforts to help students succeed. Institutions of higher education cannot continue to allow defensive self-protectiveness or a blind adherence to "the way we've always done things here" to get in the way of proven practices to enhance student learning and college completion.

At the campus level, these discussions may focus on such issues as the essential role of faculty to provide high-quality advising to students or on creating reward structures congruent with the core mission of promoting student success. Divisions may collaborate to create new organizational entities, such as the one-stop shop concept for student services. On a broader level, national research projects are beginning to identify exemplary best practices on campuses that produce particularly high rates of student learning.

The focus on changing internal practices to enhance student success rates may initially receive enthusiastic support from many faculty, staff, and administrators, but their reactions can settle into passive resistance, or even outright disdain. Such obstructionism is not unique to higher education, but leaders may find it particularly hard to address with respect to traditional structures like tenure, independent budgeting processes, unionization, and strict state regulations regarding employee performance actions.

In short, despite unique challenges, the key concepts of a professional learning community—a relentless focus on student learning, collaboration in support of student learning, and the consistent use of data to inform best practices to achieve student learning—offer a road map to enhance student success rates at colleges and universities. Higher education can and must learn from its K–12 partners and from other organizations that employ these concepts outside the educational community. Quite obviously, structural and cultural barriers unique to colleges and universities make functioning as a PLC difficult. Implementing the cultural shifts necessary to increase student retention rates requires knowledge of what needs to be done, and most important, strong and effective leadership—the will to do it!

Summary

This may well be one of the few times in the history of American higher education when external forces are strong enough to fundamentally reshape the way colleges and universities view their primary mission and their responsibility for enhancing student success. The current environment of rapid political and economic change combines with new demands to create a perfect storm that will force institutions to change or suffer the obvious consequences. Making significant advances in student retention requires campus leaders to not only recognize the need for change but actually undertake the work of re-culturing their campuses.

Effective leaders anticipate issues and questions. They can, to some degree, see the road ahead. There are many barriers that they must face in order to successfully change organizations, and this is particularly true for college and university leaders who attempt to change their institutions in ways that enhance student success. To more accurately anticipate these barriers, effective leaders study what is known about organizational change so they are better able to prepare for the inevitable difficulties of the journey ahead.

Successfully re-culturing any organization is never easy. Organizational change is a difficult, complex, and incremental endeavor. On the other hand, developing a culture in which significantly more students are succeeding each and every year is inherently worthwhile! And, it is doable. We have reached a point in which it is an embarrassment not to be able to proclaim that "our" university functions day in and day out as a high-performing professional learning community. Shouldn't every person who works in a college or university be able to attest to such a culture of beliefs and behaviors and be able to say: "At our university, we are organized into high-performing collaborative teams—in both our academic and nonacademic areas. Every office, every day, is engaged in seeking and implementing best practices—those practices that are most likely to yield positive results for our students and the adults who work here. And, since the core enterprise of a university is learning, we are crystal clear about what is expected from our students in each course, and we frequently monitor our impact on student learning, student by student, course by course, skill by skill, utilizing the power of commonly developed formative assessments. Because our teams are constantly reviewing the impact of our efforts, we have developed a culture of data-based decision making.

"At our university, we have taken to heart what we each knew all along—that each student learns at different rates and in different ways, so we have put into place systems to provide additional time and support for students who are experiencing difficulty, both in their course work and in the nonacademic areas of university life. Importantly, our collaborative teams are constantly seeking ways to extend and enrich the experiences of our students, within their classroom experiences and in each of our support areas. We do not equate enhancing student success with lowering expectations. In fact, because we have such high expectations for student success, we do everything we can to enhance their chances for success.

"In short, each year we experience more student success than ever before because our university functions as a true, high-performing professional learning community!"

A New Normal

George Bernard Shaw captured the power of seeing what we look for in others in his 1912 play *Pygmalion*, which was later made into the movie *My Fair Lady*. In Act V, Eliza Doolittle tells Colonel Pickering how he differed from Professor Henry Higgins.

Eliza: But do you know what began my real education?

Pickering: What?

Eliza: Your calling me Miss Doolittle that day when I first came to Wimple Street. That was the beginning of self-respect for me. And there were a hundred little things you never noticed, because they came naturally to you. Things about standing up and taking off your hat and opening doors—

Pickering: Oh, that was nothing.

Eliza: Yes. Things that showed you thought and felt about me as if I were something better than a scullery-maid; though of course I know you would have been the same to a scullery-maid if she had been let into the drawing room. You never took off your boots in the dining room when I was there.

Pickering: You mustn't mind that. Higgins takes off his boots all over the place.

Eliza: I know. I am not blaming him. It is his way, isn't it? But it made such a difference to me that you didn't do it. You see, really and truly, apart from the things anyone can pick up (the dressing and the proper way of speaking, and so on), the difference between a lady

and a flower girl is not how she behaves, but how she is
treated. I shall always be a flower girl to Professor Higgins, because he always treats me as a flower girl, and
always will; but I know I can be a lady to you, because
you always treat me as a lady, and always will.

Ray Kuntz, one of eleven children, was born on a ranch in North
Dakota. The high school Ray attended was small, with approximately fifty students in the graduating class. Because the school was
so small, the curricular offerings were severely limited, especially in
math and science.

Although he was unsure exactly how he could afford to pay for a
college education, with the support and encouragement of his local
priest and, of course, his parents, Ray enrolled at Carroll College
in Helena, Montana. When asked how he was financially able to
attend, Ray recalls that the people at the college encouraged him by
saying, "Come on. We'll make it work somehow!"

Ray graduated from college with a double major in mathematics and
economics. He went on to become very successful in business, serving
as chairman and CEO of Watkins and Shepard Trucking Company,
and has served as chairman of the American Truckers Association.

Recently, Ray received special recognition from Carroll College.
In his remarks at the recognition dinner, he recalled that because
he had attended a small, rural high school with a limited curriculum, he struggled, especially in calculus, during those early semesters
in college. Most other students had taken calculus in high school,
but the math curriculum was severely limited in the high school he
attended. His first grade was very low, as was his second grade, and
his professor, Al Murray, wrote a note on his test paper instructing
Ray to come see him.

Ray was expecting the professor to urge him to drop the course,
given his poor test grades. At their meeting, Murray asked, "Do you
know why I wanted to meet with you?"

Attempting to add some levity to the situation, Ray responded, "Well, I suppose you think I should drop the class. I may not be doing well on the calculus tests, but I do know the average of my test scores."

Then Murray said just the right thing—and it changed Ray's life. "Ray, although you haven't done well on the first two exams, I've watched you work in class, and you put forth an effort. And you are getting better. You just started farther behind than the others in the class. I don't want you to drop the class. Instead, I want you to come by and see me on a regular basis, and we'll get you caught up. We can do this!"

Ray had to put forth an awful lot of effort in order to pass that first calculus class. However, his effort alone was not enough. Ray, like many successful college graduates, needed a lot of help and encouragement along the way to make his effort pay off. It also speaks to the kind of person Ray is that he remembered and spoke of Murray on that special night at Carroll College.

We can, if we choose to, create the structures and cultures within our own colleges and universities that will make stories like Ray's the new norm, rather than the exception. A common story, told time and again, about the college experience goes like this: "I was told to look at the person to the right of me and then at the person to the left of me, and then I was told that only one of us would make it." What a terrible message for a student to hear at the beginning of his or her college career!

University leaders must take the lead in writing a new story—in creating a new cultural norm, one that results in our college graduates remembering, "We were told to look to our left and then to our right, and then we were told that we could all make it because our success was important." This means telling our students that they each have what it takes and that the professors are not going to give up on them. It means ensuring the best instruction from excellent professors who are knowledgeable and who care about student success. It means providing support when students struggle with issues within and outside the classroom experience. It means creating a culture of very high standards and expectations, coupled with exemplary support. It means that everyone within the university is committed to all of this, because the faculty and staff care about students and want and expect them to succeed.

The good news is that creating such a new story is within our reach. Failure to do so will not be because of a lack of knowledge but rather a lack of will and of action. We know more about how to enhance student learning now than ever before. We can choose to continue sorting and selecting students—sending messages to some that "you probably won't make it." Or we can choose to create structures and cultures that support the message, "You can do this, and we will help you!"

The issue is not whether to make a choice. We *will* choose. We can choose to do nothing and continue to blame the lack of success solely on students, their parents, or society in general. Or we can choose to work with purpose, passion, and persistence at changing the fundamental norm of our institutions of higher learning. To paraphrase the question posed by Martin Luther King Jr., When is the right time to do the right thing? Right now!

References and Resources

Abel, J. R., & Deitz, R. (2014). Do the benefits of college still outweigh the cost? *Current Issues in Economics and Finance, 20*(3).

Allen, I. E., & Seaman, J. (2011). *Going the distance: Online education in the United States, 2011.* Accessed at www.onlinelearningsurvey.com /reports/goingthedistance.pdf on December 11, 2014.

Annenberg Institute for School Reform. (2004). *Professional learning communities: Professional development strategies that improve instruction.* Accessed at www.annenberginstitute.org/images/ProfLearning.pdf on December 11, 2007.

Barber, M., Donnelly, K., & Rizvi, S. (2013). *An avalanche is coming: Higher education and the revolution ahead.* London: Institute for Public Policy Research.

Barr, R. B., & Tagg, J. (1995). From teaching to learning: A new paradigm for undergraduate education. *Change, 27*(6), 13–25.

Bennett, W. (2013). *Is college worth it?* Nashville, TN: Thomas Nelson.

Bennis, W. G. (1989). *On becoming a leader.* New York: Perseus Books.

Bennis, W. G., & Nanus, B. (1985). *Leaders: The strategies for taking charge.* New York: Harper and Row.

Berry, L., & Seltman, K. (2008). *Management lessons from Mayo Clinic: Inside one of the world's most admired service organizations.* New York: McGraw-Hill.

Binet, A. (1911). *Modern ideas about children* (S. Heisler, Trans.). Menlo Park, CA: Translator (Original work published 1975).

Black, P., & Wiliam, D. (2004). The formative purpose: Assessment must first promote learning. In M. Wilson (Ed.), *Towards coherence between classroom assessment and accountability* (103rd Yearbook of the National Society for the Study of Education) (pp. 20–50). Chicago: University of Chicago Press for the National Society for the Study of Education.

Blanchard, K. (2007). *Leading at a higher level: Blanchard on leadership and creating high performing organizations.* Upper Saddle River, NJ: Prentice Hall.

Block, P. (2002). *The answer to how is yes: Acting on what matters*. San Francisco: Berrett-Koehler.

Bok, D. (1986). *Higher learning*. Cambridge, MA: Harvard University Press.

Bok, D. (2006). *Our underachieving colleges: A candid look at how much students learn and why they should be learning more*. Princeton, NJ: Princeton University Press.

Bowden, J., & Marton, F. (1998). *The university of learning: Beyond quality and competence in higher education*. London: Kogan Page.

Bower, B., & Hardy, K. (2004). From correspondence to cyberspace: Changes and challenges in distance education. *New Directions for Community Colleges* (128). Accessed at www.qou.edu/arabic /researchProgram/distanceLearning/changesChallenges.pdf on December 11, 2014.

Burns, J. M. (1978). *Leadership*. New York: Harper & Row.

Carson, C., & Shepherd, K. (Eds.). (2001). *A call to conscience: The landmark speeches of Dr. Martin Luther King, Jr.* New York: Warner Books.

Champy, J. (1995). *Reengineering management: The mandate for new leadership*. New York: HarperBusiness.

Collins, J. (2001). *Good to great: Why some companies make the leap— And others don't*. New York: HarperBusiness.

Collins, J. C., & Porras, J. I. (1997). *Built to last: Successful habits of visionary companies*. New York: HarperBusiness.

Complete College America. (2014). *About CCA*. Accessed at http:// completecollege.org/about-cca/ on April 2, 2014.

Conzemius, A. E., & O'Neill, J. (2002). *The handbook for SMART school teams: Revitalizing best practices for collaboration*. Bloomington, IN: Solution Tree Press.

Deal, T. E., & Kennedy, A. A. (1982). *Corporate cultures: The rites and rituals of corporate life*. Reading, MA: Addison-Wesley.

Deal, T. E., & Kennedy, A. A. (1999). *The new corporate cultures: Revitalizing the workplace after downsizing, mergers, and reengineering*. Reading, MA: Perseus Books.

DuFour, R. (2007). In praise of top-down leadership. *School Administrator, 64*(10), 38–42.

DuFour, R., & Eaker, R. (1998). *Professional learning communities at work: Best practices for enhancing student achievement*. Bloomington, IN: Solution Tree Press.

DuFour, R., DuFour, R., & Eaker, R. (2008). *Revisiting professional learning communities at work: New insights for improving schools.* Bloomington, IN: Solution Tree Press.

DuFour, R., DuFour, R., Eaker, R., & Many, T. (2010). *Learning by doing: A handbook for professional learning communities at work* (2nd ed.). Bloomington, IN: Solution Tree Press.

Drucker, P. (1992). *Managing for the future: The 1990s and beyond.* New York: Talley Books.

Dweck, C. S. (2006). *Mindset: The new psychology of success.* New York: Ballantine Books.

Eaker, R., & Keating, J. (2008). A shift in school culture. *Journal of Staff Development, 29*(3), 14–17.

Eaker, R., & Keating, J. (2012). *Every school, every team, every classroom: District leadership for growing professional learning communities at work.* Bloomington, IN: Solution Tree Press.

Einstein, A. (2015). *Quotes.* Accessed at www.goodreads.com/quotes/320600 -we-can-n on December 14, 2011.

Elmore, R. F. (2004). *School reform from the inside out: Policy, practice, and performance.* Cambridge, MA: Harvard Education Press.

Fischer, K. (2011, May 15). Crisis of confidence threatens colleges. *The Chronicle of Higher Education.* Accessed at http://chronicle.com/article /Higher-Education-in-America-a/127530/ on December 9, 2014.

Fullan, M. (1993). *Change forces: Probing the depths of educational reform.* London: Routledge.

Fullan, M. (2001). *Leading in a culture of change.* San Francisco: Jossey-Bass.

Fullan, M. (2005). *Leadership and sustainability: System thinkers in action.* Thousand Oaks, CA: Corwin Press.

Fullan, M. (2008). *The six secrets of change: What the best leaders do to help their organizations survive and thrive.* San Francisco: Jossey-Bass.

Gardner, H. (2004). *Changing minds: The art and science of changing our own and other people's minds.* Boston: Harvard Business School Press.

Gardner, J. N., Upcraft, M. L., & Barefoot, B. O. (2005). Conclusion: Principles of good practice for the first college year and summary of recommendations. In M. L. Upcraft, J. N. Gardner, & B. O. Barefoot (Eds.), *Challenging and supporting the first-year student: A handbook for improving the first year of college* (pp. 515–524). San Francisco: Jossey-Bass.

Gawande, A. (2009). *The checklist manifesto: How to get things right.* New York: Metropolitan Books.

Goldring, E., Porter, A. C., Murphy, J., Elliott, S. N., & Cravens, X. (2007, March). *Assessing learning-centered leadership: Connections to research, professional standards, and current practices.* Accessed at www.wallacefoundation.org/knowledge-center/school-leadership /principal-evaluation/Documents/Assessing-Learning-Centered -Leadership.pdf on March 14, 2008.

Goleman, D. (1998). *Working with emotional intelligence.* New York: Bantam Books.

Goleman, D., Boyatzis, R., & McKee, A. (2002). *Primal leadership: Realizing the power of emotional intelligence.* Boston: Harvard Business School Press.

Gutek, G. L. (1986). *Education in the United States: An historical perspective.* Englewood Cliffs, NJ: Prentice-Hall.

Habley, W., Valiga, M., McClanahan, R., & Burkum, K. (2010). *What works in student retention: Fourth national survey.* Iowa City, IA: ACT.

Hirschhorn, L., & Gilmore, T. (1992). The new boundaries of the "boundaryless" company. *Harvard Business Review, 70*(3), *104–115.*

Hotchner, A. (2008). *The good life according to Hemingway.* New York: Ecco.

Hunt, J. B., Jr. (2013). *Educational leadership for the 21st century.* Accessed at www.highereducation.org/reports/hunt_tierney/hunt .shtml on March 26, 2010.

Jefferson, T. (1782). *Notes on the state of Virginia.* Accessed at http:// avalon.law.yale.edu/18th_century/jeffvir.asp on June 12, 2015.

Johnson Foundation. (1993). *An American imperative: Higher expectations for higher education* (Report of the Wingspread Group on Higher Education). Racine, WI: Author.

Kanter, R. M. (2006). *Confidence: How winning streaks and losing streaks begin and end.* New York: Crown Business.

Khadaroo, S. T. (2010). *American frustration with college costs reaches all-time high.* Accessed at www.csmonitor.com/layout/set/print/USA /Education/2010/0217/American-frustration-with-college-costs -reaches-all-time-high on July 29, 2015.

King, M. L., Jr. (1963, August 28). I have a dream. Presented at the Lincoln Memorial, Washington, DC. *American Rhetoric.* Accessed at www.americanrhetoric.com/speeches/mlkihaveadream.htm on March 25, 2013.

Kotter, J. P. (1996). *Leading change.* Boston: Harvard Business School Press.

Kotter, J., & Cohen, D. (2002). *The heart of change.* Boston: Harvard Business School.

Kouzes, J. M., & Posner, B. Z. (1995). *The leadership challenge: How to keep getting extraordinary things done in organizations* (2nd ed.). San Francisco: Jossey-Bass.

Kouzes, J. M., & Posner, B. Z. (2006). *A leader's legacy.* San Francisco: Jossey-Bass.

Kouzes, J. M., & Posner, B. Z. (2007). *The leadership challenge* (4th ed.). San Francisco: Jossey-Bass.

Lezotte, L. W. (1991). *Correlates of effective schools: The first and second generation.* Okemos, MI: Effective Schools Products.

Lindblom, C. (1990). *Inquiry and change: The troubled attempt to understand and shape society.* New Haven, CT: Yale University Press.

Longenecker, F. (2014). *What these college freshmen want but aren't getting by mid-year: Findings from a new Noel-Levitz report* [Weblog post]. Accessed at http://blog.noellevitz.com/2012/09/20/college-freshman -mid-year-priorities on October 11, 2014.

Lotkowski, V. A., Robbins, S. B., & Noeth, R. J. (2004). *The role of academic and non-academic factors in improving college retention* (ACT Policy Report). Accessed at www.act.org/research /policymakers/pdf/college_retention.pdf on December 12, 2014.

Magolda, P. M. (2005). Proceed with caution: Uncommon wisdom about academic and student affairs partnerships. *About Campus, 9*(6), 16–21.

Marzano, R. J. (2006). *Classroom assessment and grading that work.* Alexandria, VA: Association for Supervision and Curriculum Development.

Naisbitt, J., & Aburdene, P. (1985). *Re-inventing the corporation: Transforming your job and your company for the new information society.* New York: Warner Books.

National Commission on Excellence in Education. (1983, April). *A nation at risk: The imperative for educational reform.* Accessed at www2.ed.gov/pubs/NatAtRisk/index.html on December 11, 2014.

Nelson, L. (2014). *Big data: Colleges are hoping predictive analytics can fix their dismal graduation rates.* Accessed at www.vox.com/2014/7/14 /5890403/colleges-are-hoping-predictive-analytics-can-fix-their -graduation-rates on October 17, 2014.

Newmann, F. M., & Wehlage, G. G. (1995). *Successful school restructuring: A report to the public and educators by the Center on Organization and Restructuring of Schools.* Madison: University of Wisconsin Press.

O'Hora, D., & Maglieri, K. A. (2006). Goal statements and goal-directed behavior: A relational frame account of goal setting in organizations. *Journal of Organizational Behavior Management, 26*(1/2), 131–170.

Patterson, K., Grenny, J., Maxfield, D., McMillan, R., & Switzler, A. (2008). *Influencer: The power to change anything.* New York: McGraw Hill.

Peters, T. J., & Waterman, R. H., Jr. (1982). *In search of excellence: Lessons from America's best-run companies.* New York: Harper and Row.

Pfeffer, J., & Sutton, R. I. (2000). *The knowing-doing gap: How smart companies turn knowledge into action.* Boston: Harvard Business School Press.

Pfeffer, J., & Sutton, R. I. (2006). *Hard facts, dangerous half-truths, and total nonsense: Profiting from evidence-based management.* Boston: Harvard Business School Press.

Pinchot, G., & Pinchot, E. (1993). *The end of bureaucracy and the rise of the intelligent organization.* San Francisco: Berrett-Koehler.

Popham, W. J. (2008). *Transformative assessment.* Alexandria, VA: Association for Supervision and Curriculum Development.

Reeves, D. B. (2000). *Accountability in action: A blueprint for learning organizations.* Denver, CO: Advanced Learning Press.

Reeves, D. B. (2002). *The leader's guide to standards: A blueprint for educational equity and excellence.* San Francisco: Jossey-Bass.

Reeves, D. B. (2004). *Accountability for learning: How teachers and school leaders can take charge.* Alexandria, VA: Association for Supervision and Curriculum Development.

Reeves, D. B. (2005). Putting it all together: Standards, assessment, and accountability in successful professional learning communities. In R. DuFour, R. Eaker, & R. DuFour (Eds.), *On common ground: The power of professional learning communities* (pp. 45–63). Bloomington, IN: Solution Tree Press.

Rogers, C. R. (1961). *On becoming a person: A therapist's view of psychotherapy.* Boston: Houghton Mifflin.

Roosevelt, F. D. (2010). *Quotations of Franklin Delano Roosevelt.* Carlisle, MA: Applewood Books.

Sandberg, S. (2013a). *Lean in: Women, work, and the will to lead.* New York: Knopf.

Sandberg, S. (2013b, March 7). Why I want women to lean in. *Time,* 44–45.

Schaffer, R., & Thomson, H. (1998). Successful change programs begin with results. In *Harvard Business Review on change* (pp. 189–214). Boston: Harvard Business School Press.

Schlechty, P. C. (2005). *Creating the capacity to support innovations: Occasional paper #2*. Louisville, KY: Schlechty Center for Leadership in School Reform. Accessed at www.brjonesphd.com/uploads/1/6/9 /4/16946150/capacity_schlechty_2005.pdf on March 26, 2015.

Schmoker, M. (2004a). Learning communities at the crossroads: A response to Joyce and Cook. *Phi Delta Kappan, 86*(1), 84–89.

Schmoker, M. (2004b). Tipping point: From feckless reform to substantive instructional improvement. *Phi Delta Kappan, 85*(6), 424–432.

Schmoker, M. (2005). No turning back: The ironclad case for professional learning communities. In R. DuFour, R. Eaker, & R. DuFour (Eds.), *On common ground: The power of professional learning communities* (pp. 135–154). Bloomington, IN: Solution Tree Press.

Senge, P. M. (1990). *The fifth discipline: The art and practice of the learning organization*. New York: Doubleday/Currency.

Senge, P., Kleiner, A., Roberts, C., Ross, R., & Smith, B. (1994). *The fifth discipline fieldbook: Strategies and tools for building a learning organization*. New York: Doubleday/Currency.

Sinek, S. (2009). *Start with why: How great leaders inspire everyone to take action*. New York: Portfolio.

Sternberg, R. J. (2013). Giving employers what they don't really want. *Chronicle of Higher Education*. Accessed at http://chronicle.com /article/Giving-Employers-What-They/139877/ on July 29, 2015.

Stiggins, R. (2004). New assessment beliefs for a new school mission. *Phi Delta Kappan, 86*(1), 22–27.

Stiggins, R. (2005). Assessment for learning: Building a culture of confident learners. In R. DuFour, R. Eaker, & R. DuFour (Eds.), *On common ground: The power of professional learning communities* (pp. 65–84). Bloomington, IN: Solution Tree Press.

Tinto, V. (2012). *Completing college: Rethinking institutional action*. Chicago: The University of Chicago Press.

U.S. Department of Education. (2011, March). *College of completion toolkit*. Washington, DC: Author.

Ulrich, D. (1996). Credibility x capacity. In F. Hesselbein, M. Goldsmith, & R. Bechard (Eds.), *The leader of the future: New visions, strategies, and practices for the next era* (pp. 209–220). San Francisco: Jossey-Bass.

Ulrich, D., Zenger, J., & Smallwood, N. (1999). *Results-based leadership: How leaders build the business and improve the bottom line.* Boston: Harvard Business School Press.

Waterman, R. H., Jr. (1987). *The renewal factor: How the best get and keep the competitive edge.* New York: Bantam Books.

Waters, J. T., & Marzano, R. J. (2006). *School district leadership that works: The effect of superintendent leadership on student achievement.* Denver, CO: Mid-continent Research for Education and Learning.

Index

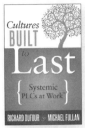

Cultures Built to Last
Richard DuFour and Michael Fullan
Take your professional learning community to the next level! Discover a systemwide approach for re-envisioning your PLC while sustaining growth and continuing momentum on your journey. You'll move beyond pockets of excellence while allowing every person to be an instrument of lasting cultural change.
BKF579

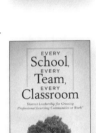

Leaders of Learning
Richard DuFour and Robert J. Marzano
Together, the authors focus on district leadership, principal leadership, and team leadership and address how individual teachers can be most effective in leading students—by learning with colleagues how to implement the most promising pedagogy in their classrooms.
BKF455

Every School, Every Team, Every Classroom
Robert Eaker and Janel Keating
The PLC journey begins with a dedication to ensuring the learning of every student. Using many examples and reproducible tools, the authors explain the need to focus on creating simultaneous top-down and bottom-up leadership. Learn how to grow PLCs by encouraging innovation at every level.
BKF534

Kid by Kid, Skill by Skill
Robert Eaker and Janel Keating
This book explores professional learning communities from a teacher's perspective. Focused chapters survey effective and collaborative team actions, instructional practices that enhance teacher efficiency, and the role teacher judgment and classroom context play in determining instructional outcomes.
BKF694

Solution Tree | Press

a division of

Solution Tree

Visit solution-tree.com or call 800.733.6786 to order.

"Tremendous, tremendous, tremendous!

The speaker made me do some very deep internal reflection about the **PLC process** and the personal responsibility I have in making the school improvement process work **for ALL kids**."

—Marc Rodriguez, teacher effectiveness coach, Denver Public Schools, Colorado

PD Services

Our experts draw from decades of research and their own experiences to bring you practical strategies for building and sustaining a high-performing PLC. You can choose from a range of customizable services, from a one-day overview to a multiyear process.

Book your PLC PD today!
888.763.9045

Solution Tree